SUPPLY MANAGEMENT

How To Make U.S. Suppliers Competitive

Keki R. Bhote

AMA Management Briefing

AMA MEMBERSHIP PUBLICATIONS DIVISION
AMERICAN MANAGEMENT ASSOCIATION

Library of Congress Cataloging-in-Publication Data

Bhote, Keki R., 1925-
Supply management.

(AMA management briefing)
1. Industrial procurement—United States—Management.
2. Materials management—United States. 3. Competition—
United States. I. Title. II. Series.
HD39.5.B49 1986 658.7'2'0973 86-28795
ISBN 0-8144-2330-2

This Management Briefing has been distributed to all members enrolled in the Manufacturing and Purchasing divisions of the American Management Association. Copies may be purchased at the following single-copy rates: AMA members, $7.50. Nonmembers, $10.00. Students, $3.75 (upon presentation of a college/university identification card at an AMA bookstore). Faculty members may purchase 25 or more copies for classroom use at the student discount rate (order on college letterhead).

Fourth Printing

Contents

To my mother,
whose entire life
was an inspiration.

Introduction

The United States, the architect of modern industry, the inventor of high-technology products, and the creator of business management is experiencing an atrophy of its industrial muscle. Although the number of new jobs being created—especially in the service sector—keeps the economy on an even keel, U. S. labor statistics reveal that every month 20,000 to 30,000 manufacturing workers are losing their jobs!

The casualty list is long and growing. It started well over a decade ago with shipbuilding and steel, followed by cameras and watches. We threw in the towel over consumer electronics, with television manufacturing the only holdout—and this largely because of Japanese companies manufacturing in the United States. Now, our sacred high-technology base in semiconductors and computers is being assaulted. An obvious cause of the exodus overseas is the desire of American companies to maintain their competitive edge by finding low labor costs abroad.

THE SHRINKING U.S. SUPPLIER BASE

More insidious and alarming is the race for off-shore suppliers that can, in fact, reduce material costs while enhancing quality. IBM's personal computers, for example, contain parts made abroad that account for 70 percent of their manufacturing cost. It is difficult to fault American companies for the 1980s parallel of the gold rush. After all, survival is the first order of business.

Yet, this short-term, company-by-company expediency contains the seeds of long-term national disaster. Is yesterday's tricke of overseas purchases and today's steady stream likely to turn into tomorrow's flood? There are already several commodities that no longer have viable U.S. suppliers. Quite apart from considerations of national security, are we condoning the wanton destruction of our U.S. supplier base through mindless individualism? And with the shrinkage of U.S. suppliers, can a similar erosion of their U.S. customer companies be very far behind?

What makes this tragedy even more deeply felt is the fact that the U.S. supplier community is not fully awakened to the threat of near extinction. For many, it's business as usual. For others, it's a cry for government protectionism. For still others, the response is tokenism, filled with bravado, sloganeering, and slick advertising.

Some suppliers are genuinely concerned, but they thrash around for quick fixes and single answers to a complex challenge. They move from fad to fad—qualilty circles, zero defects, automation and robotics, organizational development—whatever top management dictates as the program of the month. A few companies focus on the correct objectives of cost reduction and sustained quality improvement, but lose their way by concentrating on direct labor (which accounts for only 5 to 10 percent of the total sales dollars) while allowing purchased materials (consuming over 50 percent of the sales dollars) to suffer from benign neglect.

RESTORING U.S. SUPPLIER COMPETITIVENESS

Can this hemorrhaging be stopped? Can a blueprint be developed to systematically improve U.S. competitiveness, in general, and the competitiveness of the U.S. supplier industry, in particular? Can such a blueprint have universal scope in widely differing businesses—from food and chemicals to electronics and high tech? Can it apply to small companies with limited resources, as well as to large companies with "leverage"? The answer is a confident and unequivocal *yes.*

The purpose of this briefing is to develop a blueprint for restoring and envigorating U.S. competitiveness. There are a few prerequisites for success. First and most important, American management has to go back to its roots and recapture management leadership. This involves the inculcation of superordinate values to bind the company into cohesive unity; the worship of the customer over the worship of profit; and caring for employees in ways that harness their brain power, not just their brawn. Space limitations preclude a treatment of these general prerequisites. Each is critical to making supply management translate into meaningful cost reduction and sustained quality improvement.

Three specific actions pave the way for supply management.

- First is the awareness and acceptance of a revolutionary model of industrial practices that has replaced the obsolete post-World War II model.
- The second is for the customer company to put its own house in order, focusing on the importance of elevating its materials management function.
- The third is a management commitment for both customer and supplier to forge a partnership, based on trust, loyalty, and mutual responsibility.

This briefing details how the supplier-customer partnership, in its many dimensions, can be created and nurtured. Here are specific roadmaps to guide improvements in quality, cost, delivery, inventory, and cycle time. The results can be dramatic:

• Quality improvement	10 to 100 times current levels
• Purchase cost improvement	Up to 10 percent per year reduction, overall
• Delivery improvement	Near-instant customer delivery without a build-up of finished goods inventory
• Inventory improvement	From 3 to 6 turns up to 50 and more
• Cycle time improvement	Up to 10 times current levels

• Profitability improvement	Up to double current levels
• Meeting the Japanese challenge	Recapturing lost customers

These are not just hypothetical possibilities. Several enlightened U.S. companies have achieved the spectacular results outlined above. Later, we'll look at case studies to illustrate the methodology of their success.

Throughout this briefing, the emphasis is on improving the *supplier*: improving his quality, cost, and delivery and cycle times. But all the techniques described apply, with equal effectiveness, to the *customer* company. *In fact, no customer company should attempt to reform a supplier without putting its own house in order.*

How can a customer company insist on a 10:1 improvement in quality from a supplier, if its own quality practices are antediluvian? How can a customer company demand adherence to good statistical process control from its suppliers if all it knows is control charts—an aging technique with kindergarten usefulness! How can a customer company influence a reduction in cycle time from its suppliers, when its own cycle time is, perhaps, poorer than that of its better suppliers? Nothing can erode credibility faster than the image of a preacher rather than a practitioner!

The momentum of such a breakthrough, given the parameters of excellent performance, cannot be sustained if it is confined to just one pair of supplier-customer relationships. This is only one link in the long chain of supplier-customer pairs, ranging from raw materials to the end-user. A customer company must assure that this blueprint is extended beyond its immediate suppliers and to their suppliers, their subsuppliers, and their sub-subsuppliers.

It will not be an easy task nor a smooth road. We will need discipline. We will need to shed our "not invented here" (N.I.H.) barriers to new ideas. But, to paraphrase Confucius: If U.S. industry takes the first step in a journey of a thousand miles, we will be halfway there!

Table 1. The supplier-customer link: A fitness test. (The effectiveness of supplier-customer relations in my company.)

TOTAL SCORE:		
0-20: Terminal	40-60: Hospitalized	80-100: Certified Health
20-40: Intensive Care	60-80: Fit	

ELEMENT	Not In Effect 1	Elementary Stage 2	Needs improvement 3	Strong 4	Excellent 5
A. Supplier-Customer partnership: Management					
1. Management commitment to partnership					
2. Competitive benchmarking/Reduced supplier base					
3. Partnership extension to sub-suppliers					
4. Elevation of materials management role					
5. Cycle time reduction of direct and indirect labor					
B. Partnership in design					
1 Reduced part no. base/preferred parts/supplier lists					
2. Cost targeting/experience curves					
3 Early supplier involvement in specifications/value engineering					
4. Technology and cost information exchange					
5. Supplier F.M.E.A./F.T.A./stress tests					
C. Supplier evaluation/Qualification					
1. Customer evaluation and survey of effectiveness					
2. Critical component control					
3. Idea/delivery/quality/reliability incentives and penalties					
D. Quality progress					
1. Incoming inspection elimination/certification					
2. Supplier design of experiments/S.P.C.					
3. Supplier teamwork/training					
4. Next operation as "customer"					
E. Inventory control					
1. Supplier lead time reduction					
2. Supplier cycle time reduction					
3. Cycle time reduction: sub and sub-sub Suppliers					
Total					

THE SUPPLIER-CUSTOMER LINK: A FITNESS TEST

Before delving into the details of supply management, take a few minutes to complete the questionnaire in Table 1, which attempts to assess the effectiveness of supplier-customer relationships and disciplines. You may elect to do this for your own company, for your supplier's company, or for your customer's company. The approximate scores should be noted in the upper portion of each rectangle above the diagonal. Later, when you've finished studying this briefing, you may well choose to rerecord your scores in the lower portion of the rectangle below the diagonal.

The questionnaire—called a fitness test—contains a health score. The results of such a survey are a remarkable barometer of the health of the customer-supplier link. Similar questionnaires, given to several hundred attendees of seminars conducted by this author on supply management, lend further credence to the correlation between the scores and the realities within their respective companies. These attendees have often reported that their scores have dropped after completing the seminar—reflecting a better understanding of the elements of supply management discipline and its limited use in their own companies.

The objective of the fitness test is to measure the gap between a company's present practices in supply management and those of an ideal or benchmark company. Elements that score poorly can then be prioritized for improvement.

1

Getting Started on the Road to Supply Management

The introduction highlighted three specific actions that are needed to get started on the road to supply management:

- An awareness and acceptance of a revolutionary model of industrial practices.
- Elevating the materials management function.
- A management commitment to forging a customer-supplier partnership.

MANUFACTURING ASSUMPTIONS: THE OLD POST-WAR MODEL VS. A REVOLUTIONARY MODEL FOR THE 80s

American industry has operated on a series of assumptions that have guided its manufacturing policies as well as its supplier relationships. Most of these were developed in the post-World War II period, when American industry was considered invincible in its power and unchallengeable in its certitude.

But the Japanese, who have always displayed a willingness to learn techniques invented anywhere around the globe and then to cherry-pick the most useful ones, have gone on to develop their own manufacturing and supplier doctrines. This process accelerated when Japan was confronted with the oil shock of 1973. The contrast with the American model can only be described as revolutionary. Table 2 depicts the manufacturing assumptions of the old post-war and largely American model versus the new model for the 1980s—a Japanese model, which is finally gaining credibility in the United States.

The old Taylor model of dividing work into small pieces, with unskilled people specializing in only one or two tasks, is giving way to the realization that production needs a work force with multiple skills to accommodate the new wave of flexible manufacturing and just-in-time (JIT) policies.

The old model assumed that a rigid system of manufacturing was preeminent and workers had to be fitted into that system. The new model places people on top. Their motivations are aligned with the needs of the company. Their voluntary and enthusiastic participation replaces the authoritarian style of autocratic managers.

For many years, it was generally assumed that high quality and low cost were incompatible. The new model confirms that one of the finest tools for cost reduction is excellence in quality, with the quality of design (i.e., adding features) being the only exception to the rule. The whole spectrum of fantastic business gains—profitability, return

Table 2. The revolution in manufacturing assumptions.

Old Post-War Model	*New Model for the 1980s*
1. Specialized labor	1. Labor flexible
2. System is No. 1	2. People are No. 1
3. Quality is expensive	3. High quality, low cost—synonymous
4. AQL dependency	4. AQL → 0
5. Economy of scale important	5. Flexible manufacturing is low-cost drive toward smallest production.
6. Optimum inventory (EOQ) Optimum build (EBQ)	6. EOQ → 1 EBQ → 1
7. Reduce direct labor	7. Reduce cycle time
8. Optimize all sub-systems Keep people, machines busy	8. Optimize total system: D/L, indirect labor, materials

on investment, market share, and many related parameters—that can be achieved through high quality is detailed in Chapter 3.

The logical extension of this concentration on near-perfect quality is to abandon the crutch of specifying quality in terms of allowable defect levels. Terms such as AQLs (acceptable quality levels), LTPDs (lot tolerance percent defective) and AOQLs (average outgoing quality limit) are rapidly becoming obsolete as quality requirements have moved from percent defective to defective parts per million (p.p.m.) and eventually to defective parts per billion (p.p.b.). The asymptotic barrier of zero defects is no longer formidable!

The concept that the larger the production volume the lower the costs was firmly entrenched in management thinking. Learning curve theories are based on this premise. The new model, on the contrary, says that "smaller is better." Low production volumes can be cost effective with Computer Integrated Manufacturing (CIM) and Just in Time (J.I.T.) in the factory of the future (F.O.F.)

Twenty years ago, economic order quantity (EOQ) formulas were developed for optimizing carrying costs versus ordering costs. Similarly, economic build quantity (EBQ) formulas were introduced to balance carrying costs and build costs. Today, as in the case of AQLs, the most economical order quantities are getting smaller and smaller, along with a similar trend for build quantities.

For half a century and more, the drive in manufacturing has been to reduce direct labor time. The new model teaches us that direct labor time is only a small fraction of the total manufacturing cycle time and a concentration on major elements of that cycle time—waiting time, setup time, yield losses due to poor quality, etc—pays more handsome dividends in terms of return on assets and cash flow.

In the old post-war model, the theology of keeping line workers busy at all times and maximizing machine utilization was accepted as an article of faith. In the new model, these are only small elements that need to be optimized in the larger context of a systems approach to reducing all costs—material and overhead, improving all quality levels and reducing all cycle times, both in one's own company as well as in supplier companies, their suppliers, and through the entire supply chain.

THE REVOLUTION IN BUYER-SUPPLIER PRACTICES

If you think the contrast between the old and new models in manufacturing assumptions is glaring, the contrast between the old (and largely U.S.) model for buyer-supplier practices and the new (and primarily Japanese) model is blinding. This contrast is highlighted in Table 3.

U.S. purchasing strategy, despite pious pronouncements to the contrary, is based on "Price, Price and Price." By emphasizing quality, the Japanese succeed in reducing total cost, as distinguished from purchase price. Other contrasts listed in Table 3 set the stage for detailed analysis in Chapter 2.

STRENGTHENING THE MATERIALS MANAGEMENT FUNCTION

As the second action in a successful launch of the supply management process, a customer company must fortify its launching pad—the materials management function. Yet, the tragedy is that top management in the Western hemisphere has had a consistent blind spot in viewing the gold mine potential of materials management, and especially its most important element—purchasing.

Direct labor accounts for only 5 to 10 percent of the sales dollar, and with automation, this figure drops further each year. Purchased material costs account for 40 to 50 percent of the sales dollar and for over 70 percent of product costs. Further, with the need to specialize, the trend in make-buy decisions is to opt for external suppliers, thus increasing the purchased dollar percentage even higher.

An elementary calculation would show that a 10 percent reduction in direct labor costs would result in only a one percent increase in profit on sales, whereas a comparable 10 percent reduction in purchased materials would result in a 5 percent increase in profit on sales. This means that the leverage for increasing corporate profits with purchased materials is at least 5 times greater than with direct labor. How many U.S. companies wouldn't drool at the prospect of doubling their profit margins in this manner!

Table 3. Current U.S. vs. Japanese buyer-supplier practices.

U.S.	*Japan*
• No coherent supplier strategy other than demand for price reduction	• Comprehensive buyer-supplier partnership
• Vast number of suppliers	• Relatively few suppliers
• Mutual distrust, little loyalty	• Trust, loyalty, responsibility the key words
• Price, the determinant	• Partnership, the key ("family")
• Buyers are expediters	• Buyers are professional
• "Week-end" relationship	• Long-term "marriage"
• Suppliers—independent	• Suppliers—dependent on buyer
• Suppliers have many customers	• Suppliers have few customers
• Almost no subcontract work	• Much subcontract work—suppliers as "shock absorbers"
• Quality: AQLs, LTPDs	• Quality—move to zero defects
• Incoming inspection: a crutch	• Almost zero incoming inspection
• SPC just beginning	• SPC a way of life
• Cost reductions—by fiat	• Cost reductions based on productivity improvements
• Supplier training nonexistent	• Intensive supplier training
• Specifications vague, unilateral	• Clear, mutually agreed-on specifications
• Little technical assistance	• Technical assistance to improve quality and productivity
• Long cycle time	• JIT—"Kanban"
• Little reach-out beyond immediate supplier	• Strong influence on three to four levels of subsupply chain

What is amazing are the resources lavished on direct labor, while the purchasing function starves. Direct labor continues to be propped up with great organizational support—manufacturing engineering, industrial engineering, test engineering, production planning and control, cost accounting, and so on. Is it any wonder that our manufacturing overhead costs have gone through the roof, with little value added?

At the same time, purchasing suffers from benign management neglect. There are historic, but totally irrational, reasons for this mismanagement:

- Purchasing has been considered a nonprofession.
- There is a general perception that anybody can be a buyer: "get three quotes and select the lowest bidder."
- It has been used as a dumping ground for "has beens"—an early retirement home.
- It is not in the management mainstream.

Only senior management can build an infrastructure that will enhance the effectiveness of materials management.

- It must elevate materials management to a level of importance behind only engineering and sales. This means providing support, resources as well as involvement.
- It must establish an inviolate policy of buying parts on the basis of *total costs—not purchase price.* Total costs include inspection costs, internal failure costs, and external failure costs.
- It must set reach-out goals, especially for quality, cost, delivery, and cycle time.
- It must establish new measurement systems that accurately record progress toward these goals and establish reward systems for material managers in accordance with the new measurements.
- It must overhaul its cost accounting system that allocates manufacturing overhead to direct labor and change it to one built on cycle time.
- It must centralize the materials management function in terms of sourcing and contracting (while allowing ongoing releasing and expediting processes to continue at local levels). This maximizes company leverage and overall effectiveness.
- It must make supplier quality assurance an integral part of materials management, rather than containing it in a central quality assurance department, to enhance the synergy between

purchasing, supplier, and quality assurance.

- It must promote a companywide culture of statistical process control (SPC) and cycle time reduction, if the company is to be a model for its suppliers.
- Finally, it must initiate, follow, and monitor the "process" of continuous improvement, instead of concentrating on goals and results only.

A MANAGEMENT COMMITMENT TO PARTNERSHIP

The third step in starting on the road to effective supply management is a commitment by the leaders of both customer and supplier companies to a strong partnership bond.

It is a tragedy that, in the West, relations between government and industry, management and unions, managers and workers, and buyer and seller, have been confrontational and adversarial. One of the reasons for Japan's success, labeled "Japan, Inc.," is an "unholy alliance" between its government, banks, industry, unions, and suppliers. These institutions have learned to work together for mutual advantage. They have learned that interdependence is better than independence. Fortunately, the climate in the West, especially in the United States, is changing. The buzzword in employee-management relations today is partnership.

But that spirit has not been extended to customer-supplier relations, which have been poisoned by mistrust, minimal loyalty, and short life. It is not uncommon for a supplier with a history of loyal service to be unceremoniously dumped, when the buyer finds another supplier selling more cheaply. Nor is it uncommon for a supplier to gouge a customer during a seller's market and boon times.

From a win-lose contest to a win-win partnership

These short-sighted policies may earn either side short-term gains, but in the long haul, this win-lose philosophy can turn both sides into losers. The very concept of partnership implies benefits—a win for both parties. Table 4 lists such benefits for both the supplier and

Table 4. Why a supplier-customer partnership is a win-win relationship.

Buyer Responsibilities-Supplier Benefits	*Mutual Responsibilities*	*Supplier Responsibilities-Buyer Benefits*
• Longer-term contracts • Larger volume • Fewer suppliers • Consultation in design • Technical help • Quality assistance • Higher yields • More stable forecasts • Fair dealings, fair profit, fair ROI	• Trust, loyalty • Long-term marriage • Win-win relationship • Mutually acceptable specifications • Financial incentives/penalties	• Excellent quality • Lower prices • Early delivery • Reduced cycle time • Ideas for improvement • Design assistance • Standardization assistance

the customer company. In return for giving his customer high quality, low price, early delivery, and reduced inventories, the supplier gains larger volumes, longer-term contracts, and higher profitability. In return for gaining early involvement of the supplier in his design, with a considerable reduction in design cycle time, the customer helps his supplier with technical and quality assistance. As the partnership matures, the customer can view the supplier as an extension of his plant and personality, while the supplier can view the customer as providing security and continuity, opportunity, and growth.

As the senior partner in the relationship, the customer must make the first move toward commitment. (It is assumed, of course, that a careful screening of current and potential suppliers of a commodity or part has preceded the selection of a particular supplier as "best-in-class.") Three indispensable ingredients of partnership are trust, loyalty, and fairness. The following questions are a litmus test to determine the presence of these ingredients:

- Is the customer willing to share his strategy, plans, and technology with the supplier? (One leading company calls this its "open Kimono" policy.)

- Is the customer willing to stay the course with the supplier, helping him overcome temporary periods of lessened competitiveness in quality, cost, or technology, instead of cutting him off at the first sign of difficulty?
- Is the customer willing to allow a fair increase in profit to the supplier in return for continuous reductions in supplier prices?
- Is the customer willing to grant an equitable share on savings ideas proposed by the supplier?

Fortunately, the recent history of partnerships indicates that U.S. companies are increasingly investing in supplier trust, loyalty, and fairness.

It stands to reason that the supplier must be able and willing to pass the same test for trust, loyalty, and fairness on his part. He must be willing and capable of *earning* the customer's trust through excellence in quality, cost, delivery, and cooperation. He must be willing to share his cost, plans, and technology with the customer. He must not be a "fair weather" supplier who abandons the customer during a temporary downturn. Finally, the supplier must be willing to undertake a similar partnership with his suppliers and, furthermore, encourage them to form partnerships with their suppliers so that there can be strong partnerships throughout the entire supply chain.

2

The Elements of the Supplier-Customer Partnership

The next step in supply management is establishing and cementing a partnership with key suppliers. There are several elements associated with this partnership:

1. Reduced supplier base
2. The preferred supplier list
3. Supplier-customer conferences
4. The supplier council
5. The supplier account executive program
6. Benchmarking—selecting the best-in-class supplier
7. Measurement of partnership effectiveness

REDUCED SUPPLIER BASE

One of the myths associated with purchasing is the supposed security ensured by a large number of suppliers. It was commonly believed that having multiple suppliers for each part:

- Enhances competition among the suppliers to take advantage of the buyer.

- Strengthens the buyer—in terms of economic advantage over the supplier.
- Assures continuity of supply in case of strikes or other unforeseen shut-downs at one supplier's plant

However, based again on the Japanese model, these old myths are giving way to new realities. One reason is focus. It is already difficult for a company to deal with thousands of suppliers in any meaningful way with three or more suppliers for each part. Quality, cost and delivery become casualties in such a weakened span of control. As Dr. W. Edwards Deming, the father of Japanese quality control, states: "We need fewer suppliers . . . it's difficult to find one supplier who can supply the quality you need, much less two, three, or half a dozen."

Table 5 lists the advantages of a reduced supplier base to both buyer and supplier. Working closely with a chosen supplier to systematically improve quality, cost, and delivery yields substantially better results than pitting one supplier against another in the name of competition.

There is some validity to the argument that disruptions in the supply pipeline could occur if a single supplier was confronted by man-made or natural calamities. However, these are rare occurrences in a true partnership—where the supplier anticipates trouble and attempts to move heaven and earth to maintain shipments. It makes little sense, therefore, to penalize savings that occur continuously in anticipation of break-downs whose probability of occurrence is less

Table 5. Advantages of reduced/optimum supplier base.

For Buyer and Seller	*For Buyer*	*For Seller*
• Raising the level of technology • Mutual determination of specifications • Blanket orders	• Improved quality, delivery, prices • Greater span of control • Reduced Purchasing administrative costs • Management concentration	• Larger volumes, longer contracts • Technical/Quality assistance • Attractiveness to other customers • Honor of best-in-class status

than 1 percent. Further, many buyers do not realize that for most critical parts, there is only one supplier, because of tooling costs that would be prohibitive to duplicate with two suppliers. Consider, for example, die-cast parts and integrated circuits (ICs), where the high cost of dies or masks limits the choice to a single supplier.

An actual case study of the benefits of a reduced supplier base is documented in Table 6. It involves the diligent efforts of a division of a large electronics company that reduced its supplier base by 30 percent over a period of 14 months. Of course, it was not the reduced supplier base per se, but the painstaking efforts in quality improve-

Table 6. Benefits of a reduced/optimum supplier base.

A Case Study

(Sales base: $300 million; Materials base: $150 million)

	Savings $
1. Improved parts quality	
Incoming inspection: Through certification from 0.4% of sales to 0.1%	900,000
Inspection test costs: Through variation reduction from 2.5% of sales to 2.1%	1,200,000
Internal failure costs: Through less supplier scrap, rework from 3.0% of sales to 2.7%	900,000
Warranty costs: Through improved reliability from 1.0% of sales to 0.4%	1,800,000
2. Reduced material costs (Overall reduction of 3%)	4,500,000
3. Reduced inventory costs (inventory turns went from 5 to 7) Average inventory = 150 million/5 = 30 million Assume holding cost at 20%; Inventory cost = 6 million with a 40% inventory reduction	2,400,000
4. Reduced Purchasing administrative costs 9% of Purchasing budget	90,000
Total savings:	$11,790,000

With a PBT of 8%, profits went from $24 million to $35,790,000 (i.e., a PBT of 11.93%)

Intangibles

- Improved supplier—buyer technology
- Shorter cycle time
- Greater customer satisfaction

ments, cycle time improvements, higher supplier volume, and active assistance to the supplier in reducing his costs and increasing his profits that were the underlying reasons for this success. But the reduced supplier base was essential in focusing the limited quality and materials management resources on these improvements. The final result was a dramatic 48 percent increase in the profits of this customer company.

While it is difficult to prescribe the level and rate of reduction in the supplier base, experience with companies that have launched successful partnership programs suggests:

- A 2:1 reduction in 12 to 18 months.
- A 5:1 reduction in 3 years.
- A 10:1 reduction in 5 years.

Several outstanding U.S. companies have surpassed these figures.

THE PREFERRED SUPPLIER LIST

While attempting to reduce the total number of suppliers coming through the front door, the customer company's management must assure that there is not a proliferation of suppliers through the back door! Several factors contribute to the escalation:

- The proliferation of new part numbers.
- The proliferation of models.
- The proliferation of product lines.
- The proliferation of customer options.

Measures to turn the clock back on such proliferations constitute a sure-fire method of reducing costs.

Another cause for an escalation in the number of suppliers is the tendency of the engineering department to work with any supplier who is convenient—geographically, technologically, or cooperatively. Sometimes, this is done without the knowledge of purchasing. When the part is ready to be ordered, the supplier's inclusion on the roster becomes a fait accompli. In all fairness, an opposite scenario is also possible. Engineering may have worked diligently with an existing and respected supplier in designing the part, only to find that purchasing—for reasons of cost or favoritism—has selected some other supplier at the start of production. The engineer and his supplier feel cheated, especially if a great deal of time has gone into the development of the design.

In order to prevent both abuses, the preferred supplier list has come into vogue as an element of the partnership program. Drawn up initially by purchasing, engineering and quality assurance, and approved by management, it prescribes that no purchases can be made from suppliers not on such a list. It is consistent with the reduced supplier base concept and is a major element of the partnership program. It has several advantages:

- It is a brake on supplier proliferation.
- It disciplines both engineering and purchasing to stay with an approved supplier list.
- It encourages early supplier involvement without the fear of being left high and dry at contract time.
- Target costs, target quality, and specification review can be established with the supplier almost at the conceptual stage of design.
- The list provides a ready guide for supplier selection.
- It is a stimulus to partnership, resulting in an optimization of quality, delivery, price, and service.

The criticism leveled at preferred supplier lists—usually by engineers—is that new and worthy suppliers, especially those strong in technological innovation, are likely to be locked out. However, this disadvantage is overcome with the establishment of a review board, consisting of purchasing, engineering, and quality assurance. Such a board can periodically review and update the list, as well as determine the validity of a new supplier to be placed on the list, on the basis of new technology, new materials, emergency situation, or an overall potential that exceeds a current source.

SUPPLIER-CUSTOMER CONFERENCES

A step parallel to reducing the supplier base in a partnership program is the periodic conference between the senior managers of the customer company and those of its key suppliers. Selection of suppliers for attending these conferences is based on large dollar volume, high supplier ratings, and those truly interested in partnership. This generally results in a typical Pareto distribution of suppliers who account for 10 percent of total suppliers by numbers, but represent 75 percent of the total dollars purchased.

The purpose of the first of such conferences is to lay the foundation of partnership, stressing mutual benefits and mutual responsibilities. Subsequent meetings, generally held semiannually or annually, build on this partnership foundation. The agenda may vary from one meeting to the next, but generally includes:

- Customer business overview.
- Technology projections.
- Issues from supplier council meetings.
- Supplier panel discussions to air mutual concerns and to reduce friction.
- Supplier awards

It is imperative that these formal meetings be fully utilized to educate the senior managers of the supplier companies in statistical process control (SPC) and cycle time reduction as two indispensable tools by which a supplier can improve quality, cost, and delivery. These techniques are described in some detail later in this briefing. A note of caution, however: the customer company must be certain its managers have mastered and implemented these two disciplines. A supplier can usually see through the hyprocrisy of a customer who telegraphs by his actions: "Do as I say, not as I do!"

THE SUPPLIER COUNCIL

The creation of a supplier council is an important organizational innovation on the road to full partnership. Its purpose is to add the collective voice of the suppliers to the partnership and to provide the customer company's management with insights it might not receive in a one-on-one situation.

The structure of such a supplier council is generally limited to the top 10 to 30 suppliers in the partnership, with the actual number being a function of the size of the customer company. Its membership, on the customer side, includes the general manager and the managers of materials, quality, and engineering. The supplier companies are generally represented by their president/general manager or an equivalent with decision-making authority. The frequency of the supplier council meetings ranges from two to four per year.

There can be a wide range of topics, short-term and long-term. Typical examples are:

- Partnership policy formulations.
- Review of buyer-supplier expectations.
- Measuring partnership progress.
- Removing misunderstandings and roadblocks.
- Meshing of buyer-supplier product plans.
- Planning annual supplier partnership conferences.
- Technical/product exchanges (with a focus group of suppliers).
- How to share supplier innovations.
- Financial sharing: Idea incentives.
- Financial sharing: based on performance, quality/reliability, delivery improvements.
- Design assistance/early supplier involvement facilitation.
- Systems evaluation.
- Supplier training.
- Extension of partnership to subsuppliers.
- Sensitivity to vertical integration.
- Considerations for global suppliers.

THE SUPPLIER ACCOUNT EXECUTIVE PROGRAM—AN OMBUDSMAN ROLE

One of the frequent complaints of suppliers is that they find it difficult—or politically unwise—to reach top levels of management in a customer company to air concerns or offer suggestions that may have been ignored by purchasing. The concept of the "supplier account executive" program is intended to overcome this roadblock.

Each senior manager in the customer company is assigned three or four major supplier accounts. His role is not to deal with the day-to-day transactions between the supplier and his purchasing department, but to act as an ombudsman, in order to facilitate communications at the highest levels between the two companies, strengthen partnership bonds, remove managerial barriers to mutual performance, and exchange technology developments planned for the future.

In companies where the supplier account executive program has been established, success has been mixed. With those senior managers who have been preoccupied with their other functions, the program tends to wither on the vine. Suppliers soon sense detachment, and give lip service to the program. On the other hand, those senior managers dedicated to partnership (generally, the higher the level of management, the better their ombudsman action quotient) *do* make the time available to meet with suppliers at their facilities at least three or four times a year. Predictably, not only does partnership prosper, but the tangible results in terms of quality, cost, and schedule are impressive.

BENCHMARKING—THE SEARCH FOR BEST-IN-CLASS

Benchmarking is one of the latest management techniques to emerge in last decade. It can be defined as a continuous management process of measuring a company's product, process, service, or technology against its toughest competitor or a noncompeting company that is a world leader in the function being measured. Without benchmarking, a company's strategies are blind guesses. With it, a standard of excellence is determined and quantified, and intensive measures can be instituted to close the gap between the benchmark company and itself. Benchmarking goes well beyond conventional competitive analysis—sometimes called reverse engineering—where a competitor's product is dissected to glean insights into its costs or technology. Benchmarking attempts to assess the gap in overall market and financial performance, or in cost performance, or in differentiation (e.g., product quality, product features, customer service, image, and the like).

Two types of benchmark efforts are needed in supply management: (1) Determining the benchmark or best-in-class supplier for each part family (or at least for each part number); (2) determining the benchmark company, among similar customer companies, that has the best materials management function.

In the supplier context, benchmarking can be considered as a further narrowing of the reduced supplier base. The search for the best-in-class supplier of a given part begins with a rating by which an existing or new supplier is to be measured. Table 7 is an example of such a rating. Each category in the evaluation is given a weight. Depending upon the relative importance the customer company attaches to each category, these weights can be rearranged, as long as they add up to 100. For each category, there is a rating scale from 1 to 10. The rating granted is based on answers to a detailed questionnaire associated with each category. The Appendix contains an example of a questionnaire developed by a large customer company. The rating system and the questionnaire can also be used for the

Table 7. Best-in-class rating (for existing and potential suppliers)
Prerequisite: The supplier's strong desire to enter into partnership.

Evaluation Category	Weight	*Rating* (1 to 10)*	*Score weight x rating*
1. Financial strength, experience	5		
2. Management commitment to excellence	15		
3. Design/technology strength	10		
4. Quality capability—incl. SPC	15		
5. Cost competitiveness	10		
6. Service/flexibility	5		
7. Manufacturing skills	10		
8. Cycle time concentration	15		
9. Employee participative climate	5		
10. Partnership extension to subsuppliers	10		
Total	100		

*Rating scale

1 to 3: Poor or below-average competitor

4 to 6: Fair or average competitor

7 to 10: Superior or above-average competitor

(See Appendix for further details.)

normal evaluation, qualification, and audit of any supplier, quite apart from benchmarking.

As a first step, these questionnaires are used internally by the customer company's purchasing, quality, and other personnel to select the finalists among existing suppliers for each commodity. Simultaneously, there should be a search for new potentially best-in-class suppliers.

On the basis of the responses, two or three supplier companies are selected and then visited by an interdisciplinary team consisting of representatives from purchasing, engineering, quality assurance, and other functions, if needed. The end result is the selection of a benchmark supplier.

The relative economic strengths of a customer and a supplier company play an important role in the final selection of a benchmark supplier and in the viability of the partnership. An uninterested supplier, no matter how good, is obviously ruled out. Even an interested supplier may not be the right choice if the customer company's total purchases represent a very small percentage of the supplier's sales. An optimum figure would be 20 percent to 30 percent of the supplier's sales. Yet, a small customer company need not be discouraged by such statistics. If it can offer other advantages beside a large dollar volume, such as technical or quality assistance, stable forecasts, or longer term contracts, the partnership can still be built.

Simultaneous with the benchmarking effort in finding the best suppliers, there should be a similar search for the best-in-class customer companies that have the most proficient materials management function. A suggested roadmap for such benchmarking consists of:

- Establishing the standards by which the materials management function should be measured, such as material cost reductions per year, incoming quality levels, lead-time and cycle time reductions, and so on.
- Quantifying these standards in your own company with precise measurements.
- Preparing a questionnaire for use during visits to potential benchmark companies.
- Practice runs with other divisions of your own company or nearby companies.

Table 8. Supplier-customer partnership measurement of effectiveness.

For Customers

Quality

- Number of certified suppliers/parts
- Cp_Ks on key parameters more than 1.33 as % of total key parameters
- Price vs. cost on key partnership parts
- Lots/$ rejected in incoming inspection as % of total lots/$ on partnership suppliers

Cost

- % Reduction in materials on partnership parts
- % Overall reduction in total purchase $
- $ Saved through ideas/specs challenge

Delivery

- Delinquency (lots/$) as % of total

Cycle time

- Supplier cycle time reduction (wks/%)
- Supplier lead time reduction
- Number of blanket orders

Best in Class (BIC)

- Reduction of supplier base (%)
- Preferred Parts Lists (actual) as % of total potential
- Corporate negotiation savings
- Pinpointing of BIC suppliers in each part category
- Part no. reduction (% of total: Base yr.)

For Suppliers

Contracts

- Increase in $ volume/year
- Increase in contract time
- % make vs. buy

Quality

- % Yield improvement
- Outgoing quality (% parts per million improvement)

Cost

- % Reduction from base line

Cycle time

- Mfg cycle time reduction (wks %)
- Subsupplier cycle time reduction (wks/%)

Forecast

- Accuracy (actual vs. forecast)
- Number of changes in forecasts)

Technical assistance

- Design consultations (no.)
- Specs consultations (no.)
- Quality/SPC consultations (no.)

- A careful assessment of the potential benchmark companies, based on public sources of information, trade journals, professional societies, consultants, academia, suppliers and customers of the benchmark company, and so on.
- Visits to three to six (depending on time and resources) of these leading companies. Care must be taken to get information not only from the management of these companies, but also from lower levels that may have a somewhat different perspective.
- A recording of the gap between the benchmark company and your own with respect to each important standard and the reasons for the gap. (It may be that no one company would necessarily be best-in-class for every standard.)
- Actions to close the gap.
- Recycling the process periodically to assure that the gap remains closed.

MEASUREMENT OF PARTNERSHIP EFFECTIVENESS

A year after the various elements of partnership described in this section are in place, the effectiveness of the partnership should be measured, both by the customer company and each of its partnership suppliers. But the measurements must not be subjective, vague, and amorphous. They should be quantified, with tangible benefits to both customer and supplier in order to sustain a win-win relationship.

Table 8 lists the quantifiable standards by which both the customer company and its partnership supplier can be measured. Some of the parameters are logical and obvious. Others have been explained in this chapter. A few, such as preferred parts lists and statistical process controls (SPC), will be examined in depth in later chapters.

The importance of such measurements cannot be overstated. It is the only way in which the managements of the customer company and the suppliers can assess the economic health of the partnership.

3

Improving Supplier Quality—the Centerpiece of Supply Management

This chapter will concentrate on techniques that can dramatically improve supplier quality—not by a mere 10 percent or 50 percent or even 100 percent—but by an order of magnitude and more. The areas covered are:

1. The economic imperative for quality improvement.
2. What management must do for a quality breakthrough.
3. Worship of the customer.
4. Design quality—the new frontier.
5. Design of experiments and SPC—releasing the genie of zero defects.
6. Supplier evaluation, qualification, and ratings.
7. The march to self-certification.

THE ECONOMIC IMPERATIVE FOR QUALITY IMPROVEMENT

After years in the wilderness, quality has finally entered the mainstream of American management. This sudden escalation in the importance of quality can be attributed to several factors:

- A more value-conscious and quality-demanding customer.
- The muscle of consumerism—Ralph Naderism and consumer protection societies.
- Big Brother government—offices of consumer affairs at local, state, and federal levels.
- The strong arm of the law—statutes or simplified warranties, return obligations, and product recalls.
- The Damocles sword of product liability—from "caveat emptor" to "caveat vendor" and court decisions based not on merit but the ability to pay.
- Japanese competition, the "two-by-four" that awakened the sleeping beauty of American management.

But even with these stimuli, especially the Japanese shock treatment, most U.S. managers do not realize the enormous, and perhaps central, role that quality plays in brightening the southeast corner of the P&L statement!

Table 9 shows the relationship between quality and profit, return on investment (ROI), productivity, and market share. The source of the data is the famous PIMS studies, based on the responses of over 2,000 businesses. Product quality is measured entirely on the basis of customer perceptions. The quality index used is expressed as a percentage of sales, where the customers perceive the company's products to be superior to the best of its competition, minus the percentage of sales where they perceive it to be inferior to the best of its competition. As an example, if 70 percent of the company's products, in sales dollars, is superior to its competitors' and 30 percent inferior, the quality index is 40 percent.

Table 9 indicates that as the quality index goes from low to high:

- Profits increase from 6 percent to 14 percent.
- Return on investment (ROI) goes from 16 percent to 31 percent.
- Similarly, as both quality and productivity go from low to high, the return on investment goes from 10 percent to 36 percent.
- As both quality and market share go from low to high, the return on investment goes from 11 percent to 35 percent.

In all these cases, profit, return on investment, market share, and productivity can be viewed as the *results, quality as the cause.* It is the

Table 9. Relationship between quality and ROI, profit, productivity, and market share.

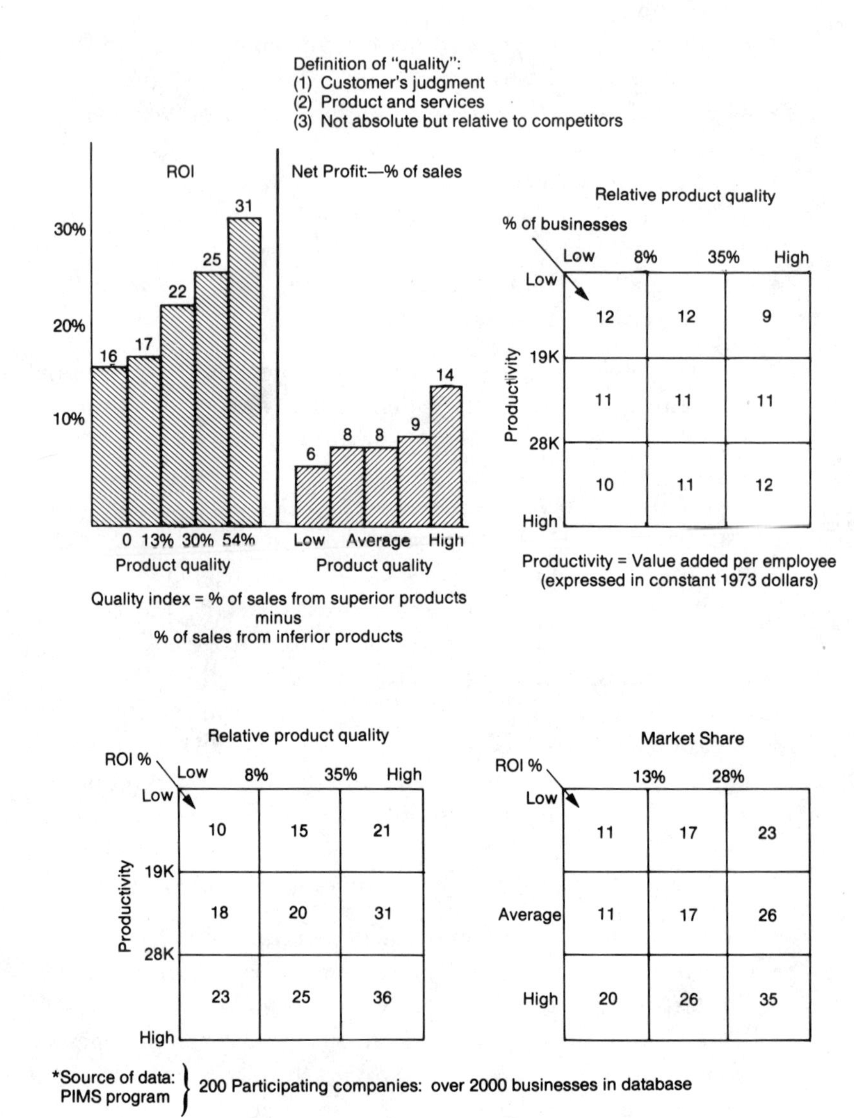

*Source of data: PIMS program } 200 Participating companies: over 2000 businesses in database

engine that drives the car of excellent business practices!

The PIMS research pinpoints other important business parameters that are directly influenced by the level of product quality. Table 10 catalogs how these parameters of business performance are all impacted in a most favorable direction as product quality goes up. Quite apart from profit, ROI, and market share, which red-blooded American company would not want labor costs, inventory, and cycle time all reduced as a function of improved quality? What ambitious American manager, either on the customer or supplier side, would turn down improved productivity or higher profits due to higher quality? And these business statistics do not even include the by-products of improved quality, such as:

- Promoting core values of a corporation to knit an organization into tighter cohesion.
- Employee motivation.
- The important reduction of design cycle time as a corporate strategic thrust.
- The stockholders' perception of the company as a desirable investment.

Yet, the tragedy is that, even today, many American managers have not seen the light of quality on the proverbial road to Damascus!

Table 10. Influence of quality on business parameters.

	Influence on Business Parameters	
As quality goes ↑	• Profits	↑
	• Return on Investment	↑
	• Market share (general)	↑
	• Market share regardless of beginning quality	↑
	• Market share for several years after	↑
	• Capacity utilization	↑
	• Investment intensity: (investment/sales)	↓
	• Marketing intensity (marketing/sales)	↓
	• Value added/employee	↑
	• Direct labor costs	↓
	• Inventories	↓
	• Cycle time	↓
	• Prices (differentiation)	↑
	• Shareholder value (market/book value)	↑

They are still fixated on the myth that higher quality means higher costs, that a shipment made at the expense of quality is the "right stuff." It is to be hoped that, with the economic imperatives of quality made abundantly clear in Tables 9 and 10, these managers will take the next steps from conversion to commitment and commitment to involvement in quality.

WHAT MANAGEMENT MUST DO FOR A QUALITY BREAKTHROUGH:

The books and essays on quality are filled with nostrums, potions, and remedies. Most of them have a nugget or two of substance along with the trivia. However, there are three towering personalities in the field who have formulated potent prescriptions for a quality breakthrough. The three are:

- Dr. W. Edwards Deming, who put Japan on the world quality map.
- Dr. Joseph Juran, one of the leading and durable authorities on quality for the last 40 years.
- Dorian Shainin, a renowned consultant on quality to 600 American corporations.

Each brings a different perspective to quality improvement. A frequently heard comment is: "Without Deming, management would not have been sold on quality; without Juran, the quality problems would not be found; and without Shainin, the quality problems would not be solved!" Their prescriptions apply with equal force to a customer company as well as to its partnership suppliers. But assuming that most customer companies are somewhat ahead of their key suppliers in quality improvement, the former should make sure that these principles are understood, supported, and implemented by their suppliers.

Table 11 lists Dr. Deming's 14 obligations of top management in achieving quality excellence. At first glance, they may appear to be in support of "motherhood and apple pie." But each repeat reading of these 14 points reinforces the power of his admonitions. There is a need to move away from:

- Short-term profits and the tyranny of the financial analyst.
- Mass inspection and accepting the inevitability of defects.
- Multiple source suppliers.
- Blaming workers who, at most, cause only 15 percent of quality problems, rather than management, which accounts for 85 percent.
- The corrosion of fear and the economic loss it causes.
- Slogans, posters, and rhetoric.

This is the powerful medicine that is gradually bringing about a quality reformation.

Dr. Juran prescribes a 7-point sequence in achieving a breakthrough for quality:

1. Breakthrough in attitude, away from control and firefighting.
2. Project identification—using the Pareto principle for identifying the vital few (20 percent or less) causes that account for the large portion (80 percent or more) of the economic impact.
3. Project priorities, based on ROI, savings potential, urgency, ease of solution, acceptance of change, and permanence of benefits.
4. Organization to guide projects—steering committees and project teams.
5. Diagnosis, from symptom, to cause, to solution.
6. Breakthrough in cultural resistance to change—identifying the cultural pattern threatened and extending ownership to the members of the culture in planning and executing the change.
7. Breakthrough in results—reduced inspection and reduced costs of quality.

Table 11: Fourteen obligations of top management (by Dr. W. Edwards Deming).

1. Innovate and allocate resources to fulfill the long-range needs of the company and customer rather than short-term profitability.
2. Discard the old philosophy of accepting defective products.

3. Eliminate dependence on mass inspection for quality control; instead, depend on process control, through statistical techniques.
4. Reduce the number of multiple source suppliers. Price has no meaning without an integral consideration for quality. Encourage suppliers to use statistical process control.
5. Use statistical techniques to identify the two sources of waste—system (85%) and local faults (15%); strive to constantly reduce this waste.
6. Institute more thorough, better job-related training.
7. Provide supervision with knowledge of statistical methods; encourage use of these methods to identify which defects should be investigated for solution.
8. Reduce fear throughout the organization by encouraging open, two-way, non-punitive communication. The economic loss resulting from fear to ask questions or report trouble is appalling.
9. Help reduce waste by encouraging design, research and sales people to learn more about the problems of production.
10. Eliminate the use of goals and slogans to encourage productivity, unless training and management support is also provided.
11. Closely examine the impact of work standards. Do they consider quality or help anyone do a better job? They often act as an impediment to productivity improvement.
12. Institute rudimentary statistical training on a broad scale.
13. Institute vigorous program for retraining people in new skills, to keep up with changes in materials, methods, product designs, and machinery.
14. Make maximum use of statistical knowledge and talent in your company.

Perhaps Dr. Juran's greatest contribution is in attacking chronic problems—as opposed to sporadic problems (see Table 12)—those that are largest in terms of total costs. Examples are warranty costs, scrap, analyzing and rework costs, inspection and test costs that are taken for granted in the course of business and get baked into the accounting system as allowable costs. Dr. Juran strongly asserts that

Table 12. Juran: Chronic problems; projects, teams.

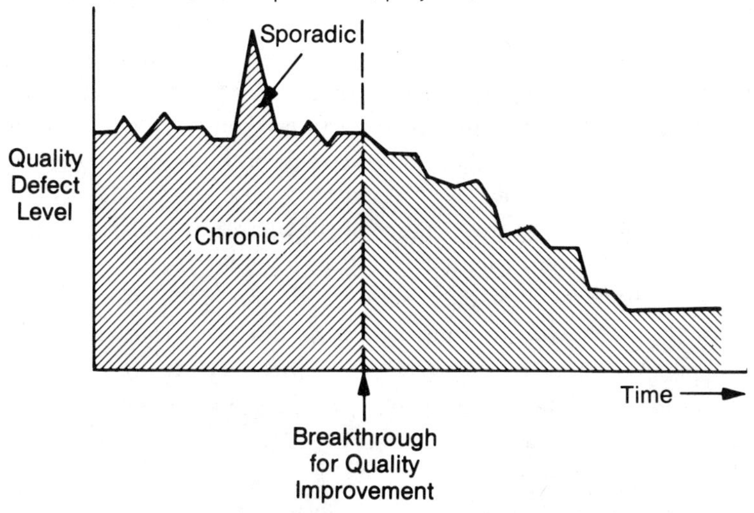

Sporadic problem:	**A sudden worsening of a defect level, with quick action to restore original quality level**
Chronic problem:	**Persistent defect, with only minor variations in time, which is allowed to fester, gets baked into the accounting system and becomes part of the status quo.**
Breakthrough for continuous improvement:	**1. Identification, quantification, prioritization of problem.** **2. Projects established by steering committee** **3. Problem-solutions by ad hoc diagnostic teams**

these chronic costs can only be attacked by setting up "projects, with interdisciplinary teams—and in no other way."

Deming, while strong on management, emphasizes control charts, for the most part, as his main statistical approach. As we shall see later, control charts have numerous weaknesses. Juran is superb in leading to the problem in his diagnostic journey. But he offers only simple and marginal methods to solve them, such as the Pareto chart, cause and effect diagram, histograms, and process capability studies.

Shainin, the least known of the Big Three, is the consummate problem-solver. His techniques are particularly useful in solving problems that have been resistant to solutions using engineering judgment, some of which have existed for three years or longer! His message: "Talk to the parts; they are smarter than the engineers!" What he means is that the parts contain all the information on causes of problems and variation, and that their secrets can be unlocked with appropriate statistically designed experiments. Once these causes are controlled or eliminated, production can be monitored with simple tools such as precontrol, allowing hundreds of thousands of units to be made without a defect.

Because of the vital importance of the Shaninin tools, an entire chapter is devoted to them. I feel strongly that if quality is the centerpiece for supply management, *the design of experiments and statistical process control are the pièce-de-rèsistance that every customer company and its partnership suppliers must implement, if there is to be any hope of leap-frogging the Japanese quality juggernaut.*

Top Management's Involvement in Quality

There is a story about a hen and a pig wanting to please their master, the farmer, by making breakfast for him. The hen brightly suggests ham and eggs. "Oh no," cries the pig. "Yours is support, mine is involvement."

Top management cannot just support quality, it must be involved. There are several dimensions to that involvement.

With the economic benefits of quality listed in Tables 9 and 10, every customer company and its partnership supplier must establish quality as one of the core values and nurture it as a superordinate objective. This means that quality cannot be delegated to the quality assurance manager, who, if he is lucky, gets to see the chief executive or the general manager no more than 15 minutes each week. It requires top management to spend at least as much time on quality as on profit! It requires an examination, not just of goals and results, but more important, of the *"process" of continuous improvement.* It requires top management to go beyond slogans and words. If such a management talks quality but pounds and thumps for shipments, the body language is easily interpreted by the lower levels in terms of management's real priorities.

Top management must approve five-year reach-out quality plans, along with similar business and product plans as part of its overall strategy. These must include.

- A mission statement on the strategic intent for quality.
- An assessment of where the company stands versus its best competition in terms of management, design, manufacturing, and supplier quality.
- A list of major quality weaknesses.
- Objectives to overcome each weakness.
- Specific goals and a timetable to reach each goal.
- Detailed strategies to accomplish each goal.

Such five-year plans should not be put on the shelf and dusted off for the following year's five-year plan, as is the unfortunate practice in well-meaning but ineffective companies. It should be a well-thumbed document, used as a roadmap to measure conformity to the quality plan.

Most companies develop and maintain quality manuals. Traditionally, most of their contents are trivial and "boiler plate." What is needed is a comprehensive quality system that can propel the company into world-class quality. Space limitations prevent the elaboration of such a system, but Table 13 is a capsule summary of a renowned company's quality system, divided into ten elements and associated subelements.

Once top management endorses such a comprehensive quality system, there should be periodic audits to determine conformity to the system. The Appendix contains an example of a questionnaire used to conduct such an audit. The questionnaire can then be used to evaluate the effectiveness of any supplier's quality system, just as the Appendix is used to evaluate his overall capability.

The audits could be conducted by either a central quality assurance department within the company or by a corporate team of quality professionals. However, the best results are achieved if this is a function of top management, as is the practice in Japan. Conducting such an audit is the fastest way for top management to: "get up to speed" on quality; get to know the problems first-hand, without the filter of middle management; get to know the people and mingle

Table 13: A capsule summary of a typical comprehensive quality system.

Subsystem	*Subsystem Elements*
Quality Management	• Quality as a core value; quality pervasiveness • Scope; objectives; organization; 5-year quality plans, MBO, benchmarking • Quality costs; quality system audit; product safety/liability; quality reviews
Customer Quality Assurance	• Value research; specifications review • Customer image surveys; customer satisfaction measurements; customer relations; next operation as "customer"
Design Quality Assurance	• Reliability; goals, targeting, prediction, de-rating, FMEA, FTA, product liability prevention • Design reviews; value engineering • Component standardization, qualification; critical component control • Multiple environment stress tests; competitive evaluation • Design of experiments: variation research; multi-vari charts, components search, variables search; full factorials; realistic tolerances; evolutionary optimization • Field tests: customer evaluation • Sign-offs
Supplier Quality Assurance	• Specifications review, trade-offs, idea incentives, classification of characteristics • Partnership program: quality improvement, warranty sharing, self-certification

with them; and demonstrate that it is willing to invest its personal time in "quality as Job 1."

If top management doesn't fully understand the economic benefits of high quality, the economic losses from poor quality are even less understood. Quality costs are generally divided into four categories:

- External failure costs—including warranty, recall, product liability, fines, and so on.
- Internal failure costs—scrap, repair, analyzing.
- Appraisal costs—inspection and test.

Table 13: (continued)

	• Supplier process/data control; destructive physical analysis; feedback • Financial recovery
Process Control	• Process specifications & measurements; positrol; process/operator certification • Process capability; control charts, pre-control • Simple white-collar process analysis
Production Quality Control	• Incoming inspection: certification, sampling plans, reliability tests • In-process Q.C. targets, in-plant data collection, yield measurements • Top 5 problems and field escape control; reliability stress tests • Initial customer quality; quality improvement teams
Field Reliability	• Packaging, transportation, installation/operating instructions • Accelerated life tests and "zero time failures" • Exchange programs, starter kits, partnership servicers • Field history & field reliability reviews • Fault diagnosis; maintainability; availability
Failure Analysis	• Analyzing priorities; field, failure analysis • Root cause detection; validation: "B" vs. "C" experiments
Quality Awareness Training	• Quality surveys; error cause removal • Quality training: for managers, tech. personnel, line workers, suppliers
Quality Motivation	• Job redesign & job excitement • Recognition, responsibility, growth, achievement • Wholistic concern for the employee

- Prevention costs—design of experiments, reliability, and quality engineering.

These costs, in total, expressed as a percentage, vary from 10 to 20 percent of sales. However, these costs are only the tip of the iceberg. Quality costs that are generally not picked up in traditional cost accounting systems are shown in Figure 1. They can amount to three to six times the readily identifiable quality costs. For every customer who complains, there are fifty who switch. Therefore, even if all the costs of customer complaints are picked up, the loss of repeat customers is unfathomable, quite apart from the loss of image that may block future customers from a first trial of the company's products. It is small wonder, then, that accounting-gathered quality costs, which constitute 10 to 20 percent of the sales dollars, represent, at best, 30 percent of the true costs of quality. And since failure costs, both internal and external, in accounting-gathered quality costs, are 50 to 70 percent of the total quality costs, *the realistic costs of poor quality in a company easily exceed 30 percent of the sales dollar!* What a criminal waste! What an unbelievable profit leak! If these costs of poor quality can be cut in half, to 15 percent of the sales dollar, profits would increase by over 100 percent! *No cost reduction in product, systems, or people can match the cost reduction resulting from attacking poor quality. It should be the No. 1 cost reduction tool in every company—customer and supplier alike.*

Top management should lead the way in driving for quality improvements and cost reduction by using quality costs in the following sequence.

1. An attack on all external failure costs, with warranty being the most obvious.
2. An attack on all scrap, repair, and analyzing costs.
3. A sharp reduction in inspection and test costs, since they add almost zero value to the product. The systematic reduction in variation described later will enable moving inspection and test from a 100 percent check to continually reduced sampling.
4. The three measures, above, should bring the costs of accounting-gathered quality from 10 percent and 15 percent of the sales dollars to less that 2 to 5 percent. Further gains can be made by prioritizing the "underwater iceberg" costs of Figure 1 and developing processes, using value engineering techniques, to reduce each one.

One of the major differences between American and Japanese approaches to quality is that in America, the quality assurance department is made to shoulder a large part of the quality load. This creates a "let George do it" crutch, where design engineering leans on quality/reliability engineering for designing quality; purchasing and the supplier lean on supplier quality assurance and incoming inspec-

Figure 1. The hidden costs of poor quality.

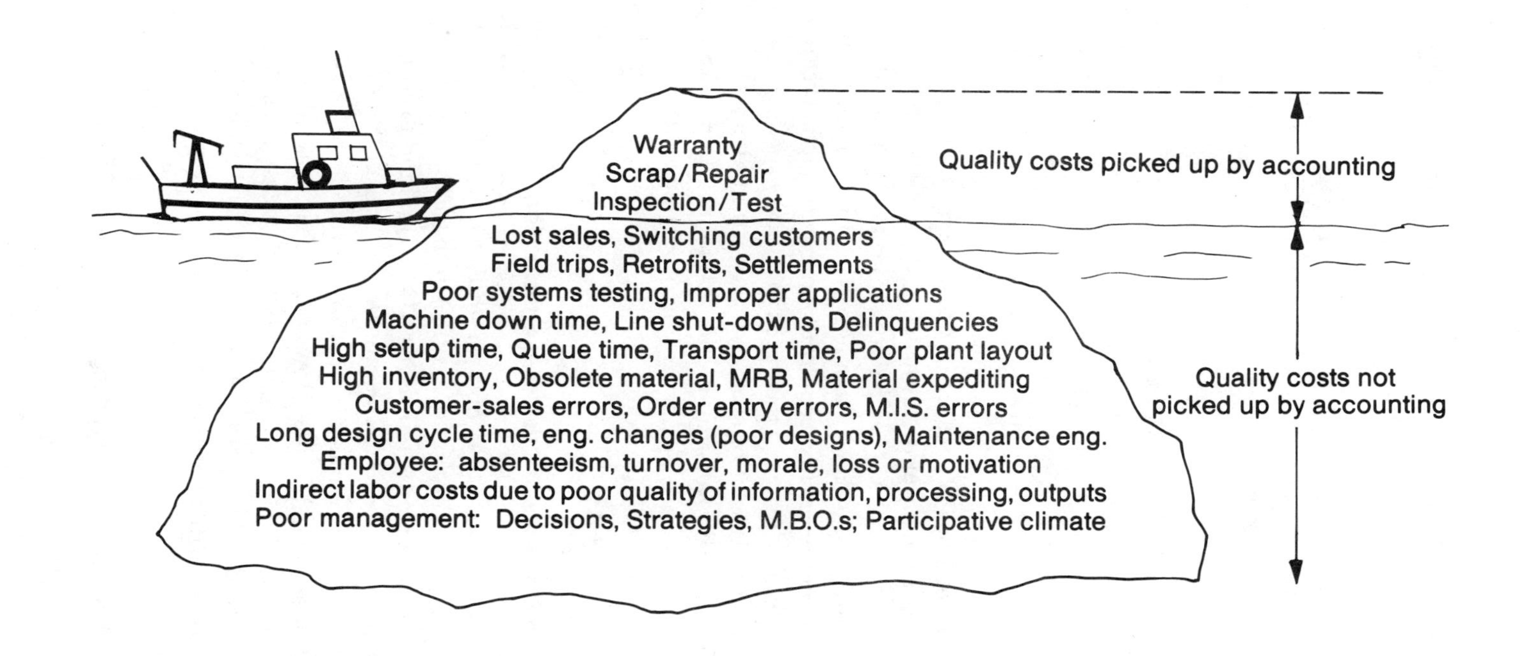

tion for buying quality; and manufacturing leans on inspection for building quality. In Japan, the entire work force shoulders quality responsibility in a spirit of continuous, never-ending improvement, called Kaizen. It is up to American top management to electrify its work force and make quality so pervasive that every employee reaches for quality ownership.

WORSHIP OF THE CUSTOMER

Many management gurus, like Peter F. Drucker, state categorically that the main purpose of a business is not profit, but customer satisfaction. To American managers, this appears like a belief in "flat earth." Nevertheless, the Japanese practice these beliefs. Worship of the customer has taken the place of emperor worship. Engineering graduates are not put on the bench, but sent first to the field to learn all about customers. The needs of the customer are assiduously pursued through the latest Japanese discipline, quality deployment, which combines many techniques ranging from market research to value engineering. Even their final measure of success, market share, is a direct reflection of customer satisfaction. They say that if the customer is truly satisfied, profits will follow. In the U.S., management tends to be so mesmerized by profits that the customer is not intensely served. This is true of customer companies and supplier companies alike.

The Elements of Customer Satisfaction

Table 14 is a network of the various elements of customer satisfaction, ranging from quality to price, from technical performance and features to human engineering. They combine to form customer satisfaction, or better yet, customer enthusiasm. No one element is necessarily more important than any other element for all customers, in all places, at all times. However, there is a law (dubbed "Bhote's law" by my students) that states: "It is that element of customer satisfaction *missing from your product,* and which is considered important by the customer, upon which you must focus your improvement."

Table 14. The elements of customer satisfaction.

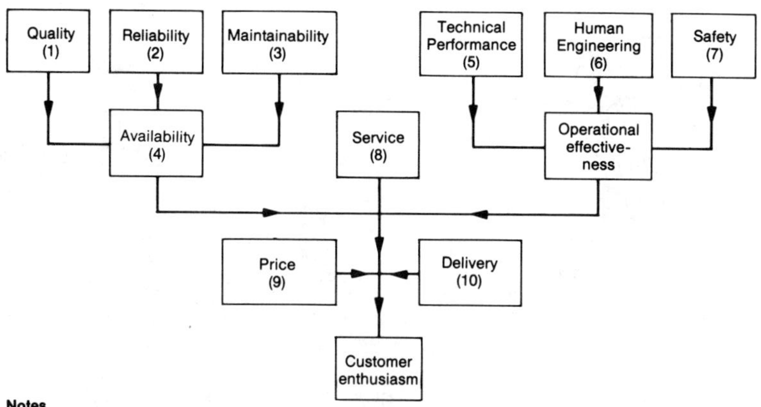

Notes

1. Quality: Time =0; Stress = 0
2. Reliability: Quality at time T and combined stresses
3. Maintainability: Accurate, timely, low cost repair
4. Availability: Percentage up-time
5. Technical performance: Features, proprietary position
6. Human engineering: Styling; color; ease of installation, use, diagnostics, etc.
7. Safety: To user, to society (includes product liability)
8. Service: Before sale cooperativeness, flexible schedules in production, full support after sale
9. Price: Cost reductions based on technology, automation, learning curves
10. Delivery: Short cycle time, flexible deliveries, minimum inventory

In order to determine which elements of customer satisfaction are being met or not met by a supplier, it is necessary to have constant contact and rapport with the customer. This is captured in a famous quote from the founder of the giant Matsushita Corporation, made to his staff: "You must take the customer's skin temperature every day." To a supplier company, this means a continuous process of:

- Determining the needs and requirements of the customer company. Figure 2 is a humorous portrayal of how those requirements can be distorted through each link of the internal customer-supplier chain.
- Separating the "must" requirements of the customer company from its "merely desirable" wish list.
- Translating customer requirements into correct factory order entries (one major manufacturer discovered more errors in his order entry systems than in his near-perfect product shipments.)

Figure 2. Interpreting requirements in each link of the customer-supplier chain.

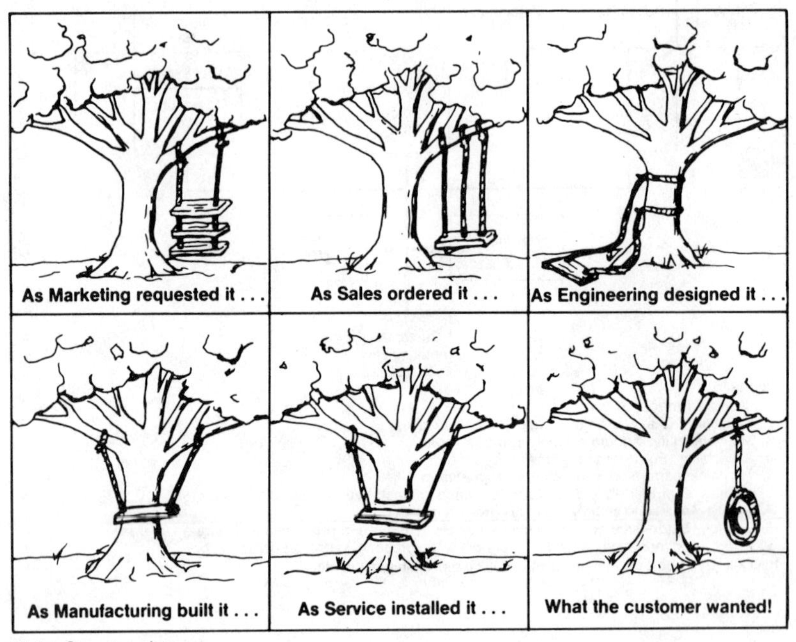

Note: Source unknown

- Catering to the customer company's need for product understanding, training, installation, service, and so on. Poor after-sale attention to the customer is the reason why two out of three customers will not return to the supplier for repeat orders.
- Continually assessing his future requirements and working jointly with him to formulate such requirements.

An important method of keeping a finger on the pulse of customer satisfaction is the periodic customer survey. Many companies do not use such surveys, confining their feedback to field reliability numbers, field replacement parts traffic, salesmen's opinions or input from distributors, dealers, or services. However, there is no substitute for asking the customer directly. Customer image of a supplier's performance is just as important, if not more important, than hard, objective data.

Table 15 is an example of a typical survey form used by a supplier to establish a customer satisfaction score. In this particular case, the company's customers are original equipment manufacturers (OEMs),

Table 15. Customer satisfaction survey.

The XYZ Corporation solicits your help in filling out this customer satisfaction survey form. It will enable us to gauge how well we are satisfying you, our valued customer.

Please request your engineering, manufacturing, and quality managers to rate us on the following elements of customer satisfaction, using the following scoring:

A = Substantially better than most of your suppliers
B = On a par with your better suppliers
C = Needs improvement
D Unsatisfactory

	Engineering	*Purchasing*	*Manufacturing*	*Quality*
Customer service: Responsiveness				
Delivery on time				
Sales representative: Attitude/responsiveness				
Product quality: on arrival				
Product reliability				
Field service support				
Pricing				
Other				
XYZ Corp. as a supplier—overall				

Comments:

Form completed by: ______________________ Date: __________
Please return in stamped self-addressed envelope. Thank you for your help.

where the customer has a multiple identity in terms of various departments, such as engineering, purchasing, manufacturing, and quality, that interface with the supplier. The rating requested was a comparative scale measured against the supplier's competition.

When these surveys are conducted periodically, say twice a year, progress in customer satisfaction can be quantified, and perceived weaknesses in a given element of customer satisfaction rectified.

Here again, the Japanese have led the way. They use long forms to extract every conceivable opinion on a product from the customer. Deficiencies are corrected with amazing speed. During slow periods, instead of lay-offs, hundreds of employees are sent out into the field to solicit opinions from customers, small and large. In Japan, the phrase "the customer is king" is not just a slogan; it is a religion!

Next Operation as Customer

The external customer can be considered as the last link in a sequential line flow of product and services, where every operation has both an internal customer and an internal supplier. As an example, engineering can be looked upon as a supplier to purchasing of information needed to make sound purchases. The materials management function is a supplier to production of on-time parts delivery. Production is, therefore, a customer of both engineering and materials management.

Most companies are trained to look upon the external customer with respect, if not adulation. But the internal customer is still the enemy, and "internal supplier" still a dirty word. Wouldn't it be wonderful if these attitudes changed and every link in the internal supplier-customer chain were elevated to a partnership similar to the external supplier-customer world! This is precisely what the more enlightened companies are doing to strengthen quality performance internally. Process flows, where there are major quality, cost, or cycle time problems, are first charted. Next, a key process step with the largest problem is then attacked by a team, which:

- Identifies the major functions of the process.
- Identifies who its major internal customers and suppliers are.
- Determines with these major customers what their require-

Table 16. Supplier/customer interface.

Program: ______________________

Function: ______________________

[X] Customer   [ ] Supplier: ______________________

Action/Information	*On Time*	*Accurate*	*Complete*	*Responsive*	*Remarks*
1. *Identify* potential sources consistent with supplier selection criteria.	1 2 3 N/A	1 2 3 N/A	1 2 3 N/A	1 2 3 N/A	
2. *Negotiate* with identified suppliers regarding quality, cost, delivery, technical support.					
3. *Procure* tooling and material required per program plan, including from samples through pilot run.					
4. *Communicate* among engineering, suppliers, purchasing, finance re items 1,2,3 above.					

Code:

Overall rating: ______

1. Needs improvement
2. Satisfactory
3. Exceeds requirements

N/A Not applicable

Discussed by:

Supplier: ______________

Customer: ______________

ments are (similar to determining requirements and specifications for external customers) and how effectiveness in meeting these requirements will be measured.

- Measures the performance of its major supplier departments, once per quarter.
- With this feedback, attempts to improve its supplier departments and its own performance vis-à-vis its customers.

Thus, each weak link in the entire supplier-customer chain is strengthened, leading to an automatic improvement in serving the external customer. Table 16 is an example, in a major *Fortune* 500 company, of the score sheet used by a program manager (responsible for new product introduction) to evaluate the effectiveness of the sourcing function. The specific activities required of the sourcing function are listed in the left-hand column. The effectiveness criteria, to measure performance against these activities or requirements, are in the right-hand columns. These are: on-time actions, accuracy, completeness, and responsiveness.

DESIGN QUALITY—THE NEW FRONTIER

There is a new realization that many of the ills of quality start with poor engineering. Most defects historically attributed to workmanship have their origins in design, in terms of inadequate attention to manufacturability. Service problems in the field can be traced to poor attention to diagnostics and repair time in design. In product liability suits, plaintiff lawyers and juries come down particularly hard on inadequacy of design, which can affect all units produced, as opposed to manufacturing errors that affect a much smaller percentage. It is beyond the scope of this briefing to offer practical solutions to each of the above shortcomings of design. Instead, we shall focus on improving design reliability, the new frontier for quality concentration, but with an emphasis on the customer-supplier aspects of reliability.

Reliability Prediction Studies

More and more, customer companies are establishing reliability targets for the products or parts they purchase, in terms of criteria such as mean-time-between-failures (MTBF) or failure rates per year. Some of these targets have become contractual, with penalties for nonconformance. But, regardless of whether such reliability requirements have penalty clauses or just targets, the supplier must first break down his product into its subassemblies and piece-parts and assign reliability numbers to each. This is known as reliability targeting or budgeting. These numbers are then compared against projected reliability numbers, based on the theoretical calculations or, preferably, the most recent hard field data.

If the projected reliability is worse than the target reliability, the few parts contributing the most to the total failure rates (Pareto's law) are then subjected to an intensive scrutiny, called a failure mode effects analysis (FMEA). Its objectives are to:

- Identify the weak links of supplier design, reliability, process, or workmanship.
- Pinpoint failure modes and quantify their effects on customers.
- Correct potential modes "before the fact" to improve reliability.

Table 17 is an example of an FMEA. The first column identifies those parts with the highest projected failure rates in the reliability prediction study. The second column indicates the failure mode, that is, the way in which the part is likely to fail. The third describes the effect of the failure on the customer. The fourth assigns the cause of the failure, preferably the root cause. The fifth, sixth, and seventh columns are a subjective rating (from 1 to 10, 1 being the best and 10 the worst) of the probability of occurrence of the failure, the severity of the failure (impact on the customer), and the nondetectability of such a failure in the supplier's plant, respectively. The eighth column is a multiplication of columns 5, 6, and 7 to produce a risk priority number. A high score for risk priority would require more concentrated action than a low score.

Then comes the most important aspect of the FMEA discipline, the corrective action recommended (Column 9). The most typical actions are: redesigning the part, adding redundancy (through a parallel path), using stress screens to weed out infant mortality failures, changing materials, and so on. Another rating, dealing with probability of occurrence, severity, and nondetectability (Columns

Table 17. Failure mode and effects analysis.

Date: ________

Project name: ________ Prepared by: ________ Page ____ of ____

Power supply Col. 1 Part name/ function	Col. 2 Failure mode	Col. 3 Effect of failure	Col. 4 Cause(s) of failure	*Before corrective action* Columns 5 occurrence	6 severity	7 detectability	8 priority	Col. 9 Recommended corrective action and status	*After corrective action* Columns 10 occurrence	11 severity	12 detectability	13 priority
L1 400 μH torroidal inductor	Open	Catastrophic. ATC enters default defrost mode. DIS inoperative	Excessive heat vibration. Defect in component manufacture	10	9	10	900	Epoxy toroid to circuit board to prevent vibration failure.	1	9	1	9
FI-Filter	Short	Decreased noise filtering of battery line	Defect in component manufacture	2	3	5	30	Corrected in pilot run (issue '0').	2	3	5	30
C4 660 μF/35V electrolytic capacitor FI-Filter	Open	Decreased noise filtering of battery line	Defect in component manufacture. Excessive vibration	1	2	10	20	Will be changed to 47 μF by development engineering for improved filter action (issue '0')	1	2	10	20
	Short	Catastrophic. Fuse FI blows. ATC enters default and defrost mode. DIS inoperative	Excessive heat voltage transient defect in component manufacture	5	9	1	45		5	9	1	45
C19 1 nF monolithic capacitor V27 output filter	Open	Decreased stability of keep-alive circuit for clock microprocessor	Defect in component manufacture	5	9	10	450	Has been changed to 100 μF for stability of keep-alive circuit at 85°C (issue '0')	5	9	1	45
	Short	Catastrophic. No keep-alive voltage for clock microprocessor. DIS inoperative. ATC enters default defrost.	Defect in component manufacture	5	9	10	450		5	9	1	45

10, 11, and 12) is estimated and the product of these three ratings calculated as a new risk priority (Column 13). This new risk priority should be considerably lower, reflecting a significant improvement in projected reliability on the parts with the highest failure rates in the reliability prediction study.

FTA and PLA

Two reliability disciplines, allied to FMEA, are fault tree analysis (FTA) and product liability analysis (PLA). The first, FTA, is a mirror image of FMEA. In the latter, the study starts with a failed part and estimates its consequences to the customer. In FTA, the start is with a failure in the system that a customer is likely to see; its several possible causes are then traced in an organized trouble-shooting manner. The objective is to review all paths to failure in order to anticipate and correct them "before the fact."

Product liability analysis is the newest of the reliability disciplines introduced because of the extreme danger of product liability suits, where unscrupulous plaintiff lawyers sue everybody—dealers, distributors, manufacturers, suppliers, and *their* suppliers—on and on through the whole supply chain. Court judgments and the huge and totally unreasonable fines levied have spawned a "sue" culture, from which no one, manufacturer or supplier, is immune. The product liability analysis (PLA) is one of the best exhibits in court by which a manufacturer or supplier can defend the integrity of his design. The PLA study is similar to an FTA, but confined to only those field failures likely to cause user injury. The more thorough of the PLA studies include a rating (probability of failure multiplied by its severity) for each branch of the PLA tree. Space limitations prevent a detailed treatment of FTAs and PLAs. The reader is referred to the considerable volume of literature on these subjects.

Multiple Environment Overstress Tests

Reliability prediction, FMEA, FTAs, and PLAs are only paper studies and projections. The real assessment of reliability is through actual tests on the product, either at the customer company's facility or, preferably, at the supplier company. Traditionally, even the better companies do this with tests involving each environment or stress performed singly and sequentially. There are severe limitations on this method of stress testing:

- In the field—the real world—stresses and environments do not impinge upon a product one at a time. Therefore, by not combining these environments, the all-important interaction effects, where environments act in unison and with synergy, are missed.
- Under these conditions, the correlation with the eventual field failure rates, that the practitioners of single environment, sequential testing claim, is more hope and prayer than reality. In fact, repeated tests of the same product do not produce the same projected failure rates.
- Most important, these tests do not weed out those potential failures that lie above the domain of arbitrary stress specifications.

In multiple environment overstress testing* (MEOST), the objective is nothing short of zero failures in reliability, just as the objective of statistical process control and the design of experiments is zero defects in design/production quality. The methodology of MEOST is outlined in Table 18 and Figure 3. (It assumes that the practitioner is familiar with conventional Weibull plots and analysis). Experience says MEOST can detect potential field failures that single environment sequential testing cannot. These failures are of the same type (same failure mode and mechanism) that are found in the field, based on history. Further, the actual test times required for MEOST as well as the number of test units are considerably less than for single environment sequential tests.

Classification of Characteristics

Another important element in the supplier-customer aspects of design quality is the classification of characteristics—or parameters—in drawings or specifications given to suppliers.

*The principles and practice of MEOST have been developed by Dorian Shainin, who has used it to vastly improve the reliability of products ranging from simple parts to helicopters to the lunar module—the only space hardware that has never failed!

Table 18. Multiple environment overstress test: A roadmap

1. Prioritize customer specifications, including applications, environments, etc.,
2. Test 40 units in the field under varying environment/stress conditions and monitor levels with appropriate instrumentation.
3. Plot a frequency distribution of levels for each environment/stress.
4. Establish the limits for each level that includes 39 out of 40 readings (2.5% tail). These limits become the design stress levels.
5. Combine all environments/stresses up to the maximum level determined in Step 4.
6. Select a sample of units (minimum 10, maximum 30), representative of the design being evaluated, and subject it to the combined stresses established in Step 4 for a fraction of the total service life of the product (Δt_1 in Figure 3).
7. If failures occur within this limited "operating rectangle," discontinue testing, analyze figures, and strengthen the design.
8. If there are no failures, continue to time stress the units, beyond the design stress level, on a combined stress and time scale until a maximum practical overstress level is reached.
9. If failures occur, determine if the failure mode (or modes) is artificial (i.e., not likely under actual field conditions) or realistic.
10. Ignore the failures, if the failure mode is artificial or, if realistic, there are three or fewer figures of a particular failure mechanism.
11. If four or more realistic failures of the same failure mode and same failure mechanism occur, plot the failure points (1% failures vs. stress time on Weibull paper). Connect the failure points and project down to a 1% failure point.
12. If this 1% failure point falls inside the operating rectangle, stop the testing, analyze the root cause of the failures, and change the design or materials.
13. If the 1% failure point falls outside the operating rectangle, continue testing with another set of units for a larger fraction of the total service life (Δt_2 in Figure 3).
14. Repeat steps 7 through 12. If the 1% failure point falls outside the operating rectangle, the product is given qualified approval to go into production.
15. In cooperation with the customer, retrieve a few units from the field that have known operating times, and test these units in the same manner (Δt_3, Δt_4, etc.). It would be desirable to repeat this test with increasing field times. If the 1% failure point clears the operating rectangle, the product can be considered to give the highest reliability that can be achieved.

Figure 3. A brief roadmap of multiple environment overstress testing.

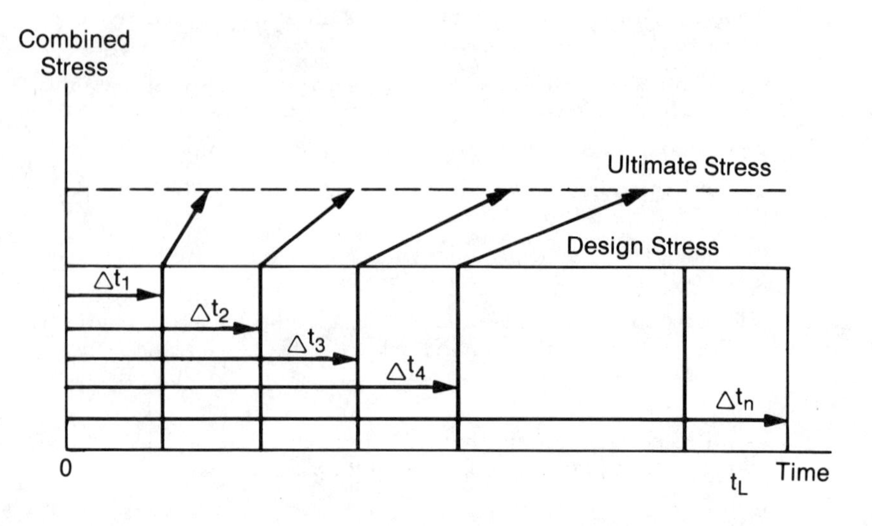

The traditional approach has been to look upon all characteristics as equally important and to hold the supplier responsible for meeting all of them. Incoming inspection may or may not be told what characteristics are important and what are not, but the supplier is kept in the dark and his feet are held to the fire to assure 100 percent compliance with all parameters.

The quality approach recognizes that all specifications are not equally important. The classification of characteristics means that only the important specifications, from a function viewpoint, are singled out for special supplier attention. These are the areas that must have zero AQLs (acceptable quality levels) in the customer's incoming inspection. These are the areas that must have a minimum C_{PK} of 1.33, and preferably C_{PK}s of 2, 5, and more, without adding cost. In fact, if done right, these high C_{PK}s will reduce costs. These are the areas that must have their variability reduced through the design of experiments. The other parameters, which engineering uses mainly as "information added" or "hide protectors" for insecure engineers, can easily be deemphasized.

DESIGN OF EXPERIMENTS AND SPC—RELEASING THE GENIE OF ZERO DEFECTS!

Nothing is more distressing than our dismal understanding of two of the newer quality disciplines, design of experiments (DOE) and statistical process control (SPC). Figure 4 displays quality progress, as a percentage of a hypothetical ideal, versus time. It shows the lead the U.S. had after World War II dissipating by the mid-1960s, with Japan widening the gap ever since.

However, when the three components of total quality—the traditional approach, SPC, and DOE—are considered, the gap is even more alarming. The traditional approach to quality consists of old and worn techniques such as inspection, sampling plans, correction and detection (over-prevention), delegation of quality responsibility to a detached professional group, and so on. Figure 4 shows that Japan abandoned this traditional approach in the 60s, while the United States strove to make quality headway the hard way, with the use of these obsolete tools until the 80s.

SPC in Japan—"Too Little and Too Late"

As a result of Deming, Juran, and other U.S. trainers (this author played a role in the quality training of his company's Japanese joint venture and suppliers), Japan launched SPC and rode its crest till 1980, when it came to the realization that even SPC in production was "too little and too late." In the United States, SPC, learned during World War II, was considered passé, but was reembraced in 1980, about the same time that the Japanese were moving away from it. A watershed mark in the United States between traditional quality control and SPC was the famous NBC *White Paper*—"If Japan Can, Why Can't We?" It elevated W. Edward Deming to the status of a prophet in his own land and the SPC bandwagon started to roll. Unfortunately, SPC in this country is largely equated with nothing more than control charts. As we shall examine later in this chapter, control charts are complex, wasteful, and limited in their diagnostic power to reduce variability! The Japanese learned this lesson many years ago. For all practical purposes, they have abandoned the use of control charts, except as show-and-tell for visiting American firemen.

Figure 4. Contribution of traditional, SPC, and design of experiments tools to quality progress.

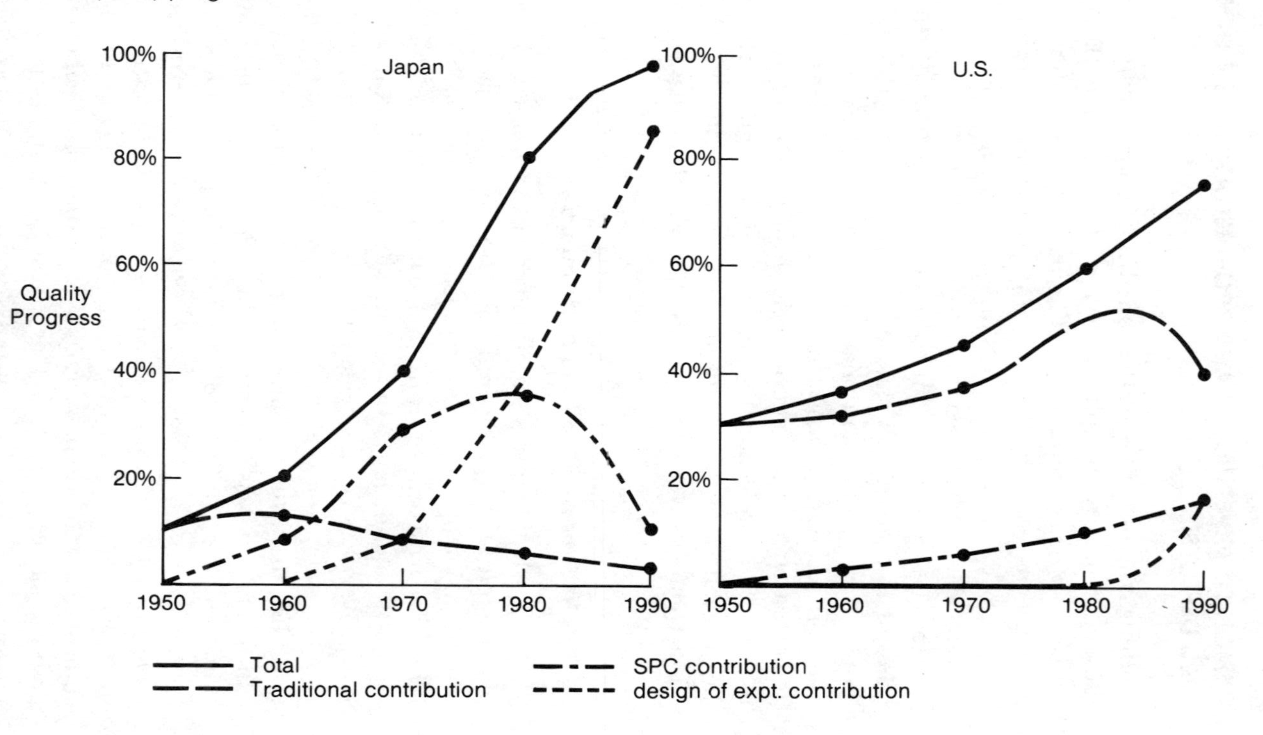

Design of Experiments—Japan's Secret Weapon

The central thrust, and secret weapon, of Japanese quality is the extensive use of design of experiments (DOE), whereby variability in the design of products and processes can be drastically reduced before unit No. 1 is in production. DOE in Japan started with Dr. Genichi Taguchi's Orthogonal Array, an adaptation of the classical design of experiments fathered by Sir Ronald Fisher in Britain. Today, hundreds of Japanese companies conduct thousands of designed experiments each year to reduce variability.

Except for a small band of companies and academics, DOE was practically unheard of in U.S. corporations. A belated movement started in the early 1980s, but it is mesmerized by the Taguchi name. The irrational logic is that if it is Japanese, it has to be good. Yet, the Taguchi orthogonal array has many serious drawbacks:

- It is complicated. Engineers are uncomfortable even with simple statistical concepts such as standard deviation, and much more so with analysis of variance.
- It is expensive. With inner arrays and outer arrays multiplied together, the number of experiments can go up to several hundred.
- The orthogonal array belongs in the family of fraction factorials, and suffers from the same statistical flaws as that generic family, namely confounding of interaction effects (especially higher order interaction effects) with main effects.
- It does not believe in randomization—a cardinal statistical sin.
- It gives sub-optimal results, with apparent benefits that can be reversed later.

The Shainin Diagnostic Tools—Simple, Pervasive, Powerful

Fortunately for America, Dorian Shainin—along with his fundamental contribution to reliability perfection through multiple environment overstress testing—has given us his DOE tools that can diagnose and correct the causes of variation and lead us beyond zero defects to zero variability in quality. These tools are:

- *Simple,* understood by engineers and line workers alike. The mathematics involved is unbelievably elementary.
- *Logical*—they are based on common sense.
- *Practical*—easy to implement.
- *Universal in scope,* applicable to a wide range of industries, both process-intensive and assembly-intensive.
- *Statistically powerful* in terms of accuracy, with no violations of statistical principles.
- *Excellent in terms of results,* with quality gains not in the 10-30 percent range, but in the 100 to 1000 percent range.

These powerful Shainin tools can enable America to beat the Japanese at their own game of design quality. Yet the sad truth is that most American companies are unaware of their existence!

Before describing the Shainin diagnostic tools, variation needs to be quantified. In just-in-time (JIT) practices, inventory is considered evil. In quality, variation is evil. In fact, quality control, from this view point, can be defined as the systematic identification analysis, reduction, and eventual elimination of variation. With this definition, specification limits that have controlled our industrial lives are no longer adequate. Figure 5 shows the conventional American view that if a unit falls within specification limits, 100 percent customer satisfaction is assumed, with no economic loss in production. The Japanese view differs sharply from that perception. Any departure from a target or design center of a quality characteristic represents an economic loss because: (1) customers get progressively dissatisfied as a product approaches the marginal limits of acceptance and as they perceive lack of uniformity from unit to unit, even though each unit may be within specification limits; and (2) internal manufacturing costs increase as the factory strains to bring units into specification limits. These result from scrap, analyzing, and repair costs, and often inspection/test costs that add no value to the product.

An analogy can be drawn from school grades. If a student gets a D and passes, and another gets an E and fails, there is really not much difference between them. They are both marginal students, at best. What is needed is to bring all students close to an A grade, just as we want all units to come close to design center.

Figure 5. Specifications limits vs. target values.

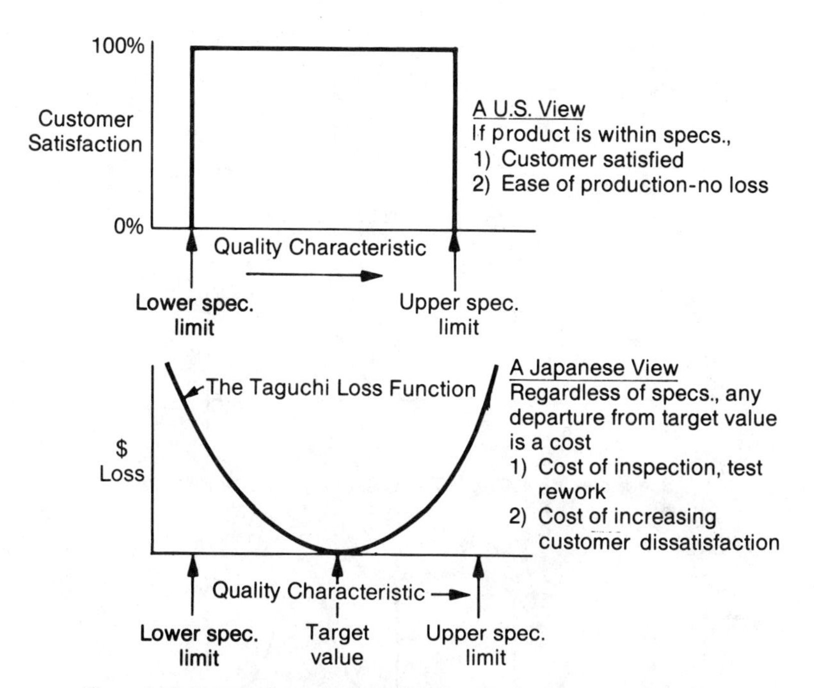

Taguchi interpretation of a specification limit
That value where external costs at customer (including loss of sales, warranty, etc.) equal internal costs (inspection, test, analyzing, rework)

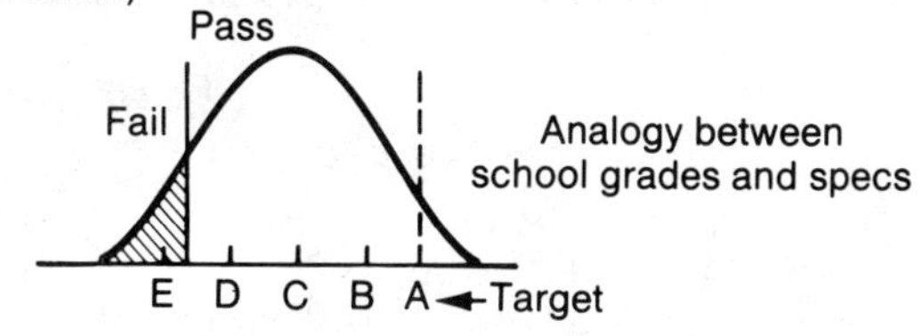

Figure 6 shows various distributions of process limits relative to specification limits. A simple way to define a process capability index

Figure 6. Process capability index examples.

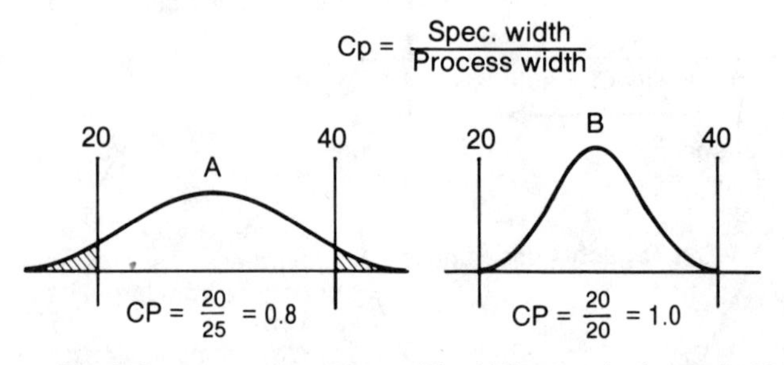

The U.S. norm in the 1970s

The U.S. norm in the early 1980s

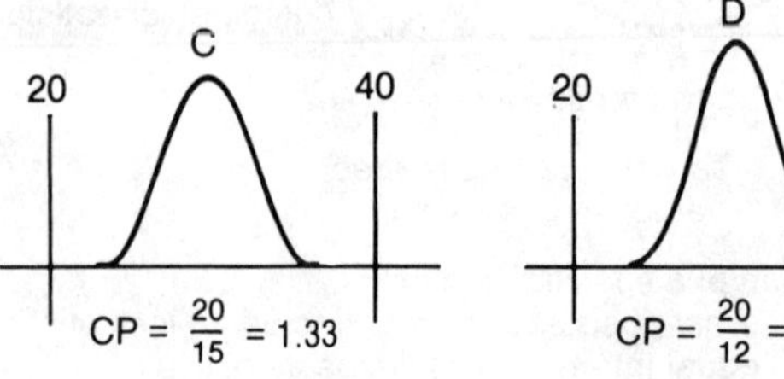

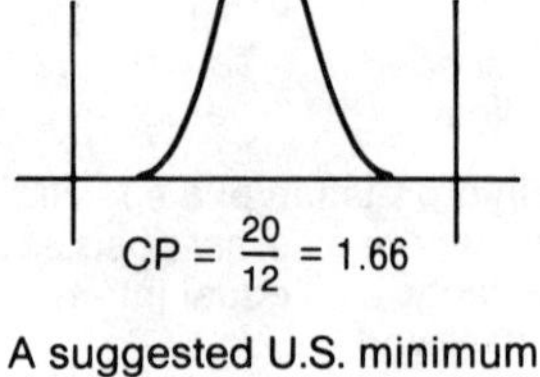

The Japanese minimum

A suggested U.S. minimum

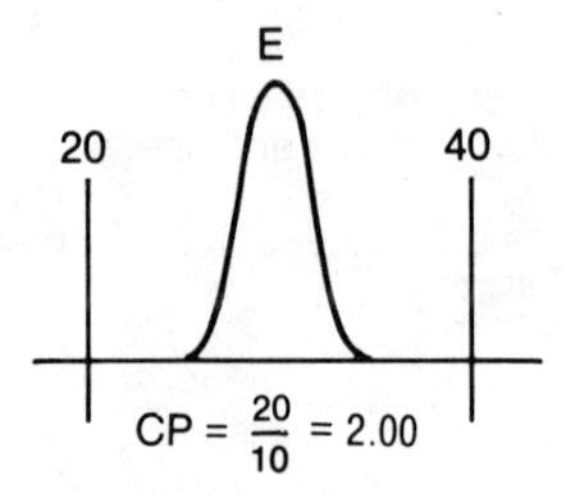

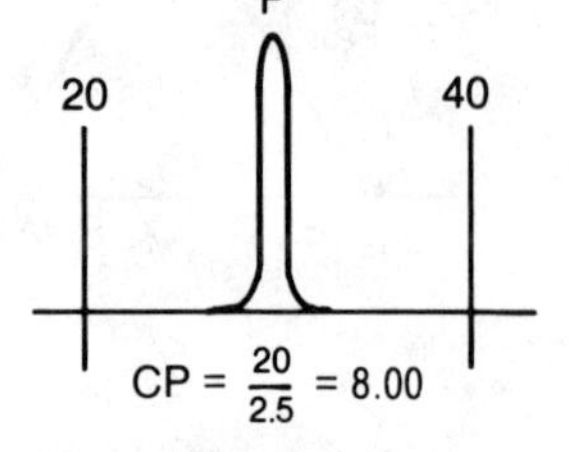

A suggested U.S. norm

An ideal
(with no increase
in costs)

is Cp, which is equal to the specifications width (of a given quality characteristic) divided by process width.

Process A in Figure 6 is out of control, showing reject tails at both ends. Its Cp is less than unity. It was the norm for U.S. processes in the 1970s. Process B is barely in control. Its Cp is unity. It is typical of U.S. processes in the early 1980s, before the introduction of SPC. Process C, with a Cp of 1.33 has a margin of safety between the specification limit and the process limit of each side. The Japanese use this as a minimum for important processes. Process D, with a Cp of 1.66, is suggested as a minimum U.S. standard, while process E, with a Cp of 2.0, is recommended as a U.S. norm. Process F, with a Cp of 8.0, is ideal. It can be and has been achieved in several leading U.S. companies (including the author's) *without adding costs.* As a matter of fact, with such high Cps, not only are scrap, analyzing, and repair costs zero, but inspection and test can be reduced from 100 percent to sample test and even eliminated.

Cp is used only as a simple introduction to the concept of process capability. It does not take into account any noncentering of the process relative to the specification limits of a quality characteristic. Such noncentering reduces the margin of safety and therefore has a penalty imposed, called a "K" or correction factor. The formula for K is:

$$K = (1)\,\frac{D - \overline{X}}{w/2} \text{ or } (2)\,\frac{\overline{X} - D}{w/2}$$ (use formula (1) or (2) so that K is always positive)

Where D is the design center or target

$\overline{X}$ is the process average

w is the specification width

The process capability index (Cp_K) is then defined as:

$Cp_K = (1 - K)\,Cp.$

By virtue of the above formulas, when the process is centered, that is, when the design center, D, and the process average $\overline{X}$, coincide, K is reduced to zero. This means that when a process is centered $Cp = Cp_K$.

Figure 7 shows four examples of frequency distributions. A is a

Figure 7. Process capability index: C_{P_K}

$$C_P = \frac{\text{Spec. width (w)}}{\text{Process width}} \; : \; C_{P_K} = (1\text{-}K)C_P \; ; \; K = \frac{\text{Design center (D)} - \overline{X}^*}{w/2}$$

*Ignore a minus figure in the numerator

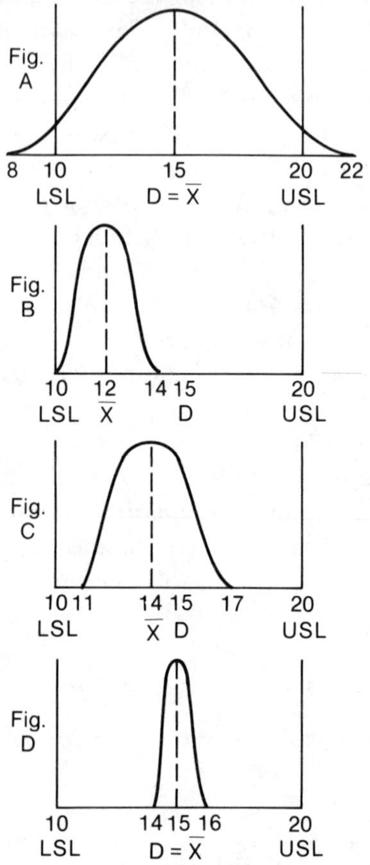

Fig. A

8 10 LSL — 15 $D = \overline{X}$ — 20 USL 22

$C_P = C_{P_K} = 0.71$
Typical Process capability till early 1980s

Fig. B

10 LSL — 12 $\overline{X}$ — 14 15 D — 20 USL

$C_P = 2.5$; $C_{P_K} = 1.0$
Despite narrow distribution, poor C_{P_K} because $\overline{X}$ far from design center

Fig. C

10 11 LSL — 14 15 $\overline{X}$ D — 17 — 20 USL

$C_P = 1.67$; $C_{P_K} = 1.33$
Wider distribution than Fig. B, but closer to design center, so acceptable C_{P_K}

Fig. D

10 LSL — 14 15 16 $D = \overline{X}$ — 20 USL

$C_P = C_{P_K} = 5$
Ideal distribution

For critical parameters: Minimum $C_{P_K} = 1.33$
Desirable $C_{P_K} = 2.00$
Ideal $C_{P_K} = 5.00$

Code

LSL = Lower spec. limit
USL = Uper spec. limit
W = Spec. width
D = Design center (or target)
$\overline{x}$ = Process average
K =Correction factor for noncentered distribution

process that is out of control and producing defects. It has a poor Cp_K, less than unity. B has a narrow distribution with a good Cp of 2.5. But because it is close to one specification limit and in danger of producing defects, its Cp_K is penalized and reduced to 1.0. C has a wider distribution than B and hence, a lower Cp of 1.67. Partly because it is better centered than B, it pays a lesser penalty, a Cp_K of 1.33. D is the ideal and has both a narrow distribution and a centered process, giving it a Cp_K of 5.0.

For important processes, in both supplier and customer companies, the following Cp_Ks are recommended.

- Minimum Cp_Ks: 1.33
- Desirable Cp_K: 2.00
- Ideal Cp_K: 5 and over

Experience shows, however, that with the Shainin variation reduction techniques, Cp_Ks of 10 and even 20 are attained at no extra cost. Under such conditions, parts can be put together in production with no scrap and rework, and little inspection and test.

But if a product, new or old, has a large variation, that is, a low Cp_K, there is a systematic way to reduce variation and increase Cp_K using the Shainin diagnostic tools. To describe each one in detail would require a separate briefing (which this author is preparing). It is hoped, however, that by providing a brief synopsis of each technique, the reader will be stimulated to probe further and become a champion of this methodology in his own company and in his suppliers' companies. Figure 8 is a roadmap of the diagnostic journey. The analogy of a detective story is suggested, where the object is to gather clues, each progressively more positive, until the culprit cause, or input variable, which contributes most to variation is apprehended, reduced, and controlled. In the Shainin lexicon, the culprit variable is the Red X, the second most important cause is called the Pink X, the third, the Pale Pink X.

Table 19 describes each of the tools of Figure 8—its objective and methodology. Again, because of space limitations, only one Shainin tool, Variables Search, will be explained in some detail. It is America's leap-frogging answer to Taguchi and DOE in Japan.

Figure 8. Design of experiments/statistical process control: a roadmap

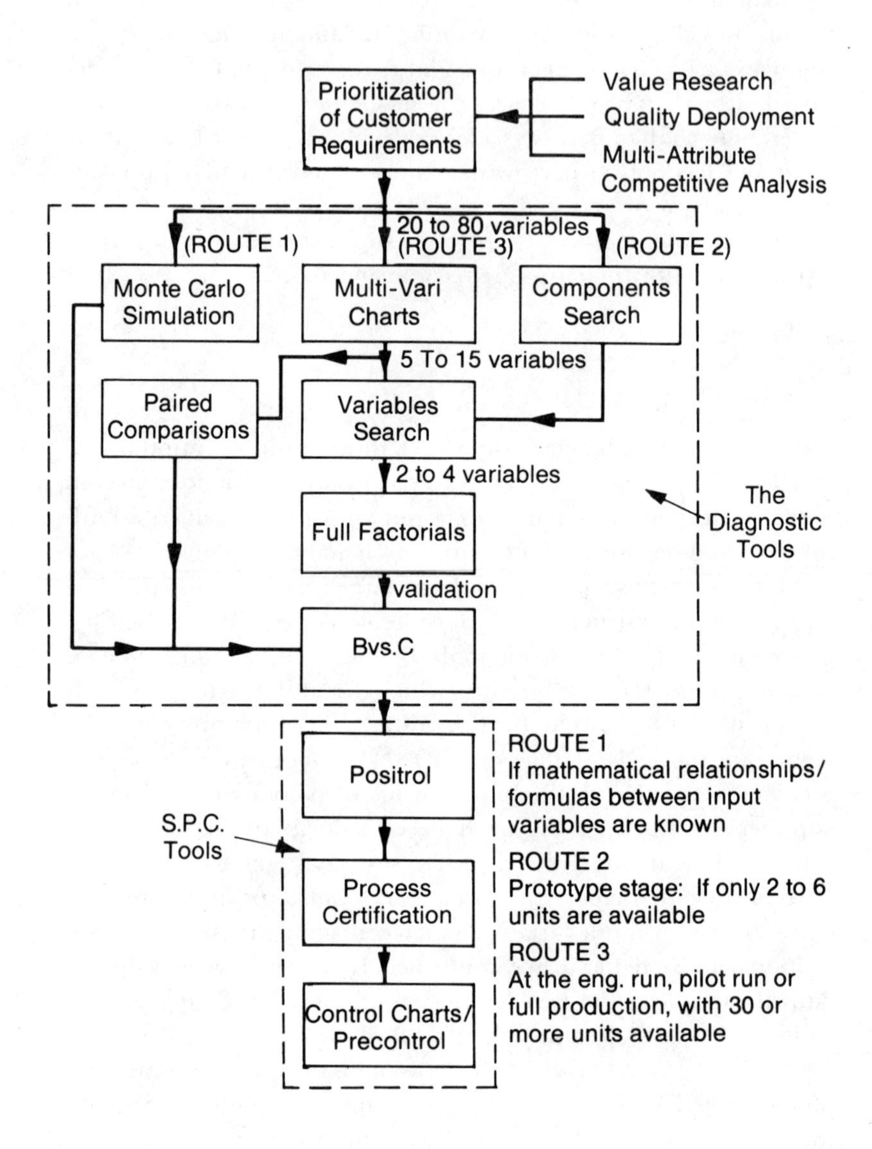

Table 19. The diagnostic journey to the Red X.

Tool	*Objective*	*Brief Methodology*
Value research Multi-attribute analysis	Prioritize customer requirements.	1. Prioritize customer's perceptions of differentiation parameters—quality, features, service—by importance and by relative position vis-à-vis competition. 2. Translate into realistic product specifications.
Monte Carlo simulation	Determine optimum values/tolerances of components of a design.	(Not a Shanin technique—and only useful if mathematical relationships between variables are known). Iterative computer passes at values/tolerances of each component to optimize a given output.
Components search (particularly useful when only a few units are available in prototype stage)	Home in on a few key variables from a wide variety of variables to capture the family of the Red X or the Red X itself. (Applications mainly in assembly work).	1. Take two units (usually assemblies)—one good, one bad. Output difference should be 5:1. 2. Swap suspect subassemblies or components between good and bad units. If bad unit becomes good, Red X family or Red X is captured. If not, continue swaps of other subassemblies or components until search is narrowed. 3. Components must be returned to original assembly to see if original difference is verified. 4. If there are two or more causes of the problem, look for interactions (based upon partial reversals) and analyze.

Table 19 (continued). The diagnostic journey to the Red X.

Tool	*Objective*	*Brief Methodology*
Multi-vari charts	1. Discover family of Red X —time, cycle, or position. 2. Improve process capability by 50 to 80.	1. Take stratified samples of consecutive items at different times—e.g., within unit, unit-to-unit, time-to-time. Plot output on chart. 2. Examine chart visually (or arithmetically) to determine which variation is largest—time, cycle, or position. Also look for nonrandom patterns. 3. Family of Red X now known.
Paired comparisons	1. Detect significant differences between good and bad units, when disassembly and reassembly cannot be performed. 2. Provide strong clues to the Red X.	1. Select one good and one bad unit in production. Observe differences—visual, chemical, physical. 2. Repeat on 5 or 6 more such pairs of good and bad units. 3. Search for repetitions in observed differences among these pairs. These repetitions provide major clues to the probable Red X.
Variables search	See next section for detailed treatment.	See next section for detailed treatment.
Full factorials	1. Obtain quantified estimates of the magnitude of the main and interaction effects of the selected variables upon the output. 2. Home in on the Red X, following a multi-vari chart, if no more than four variables are investigated.	1. Set up a matrix of experiments involving four or fewer variables at two levels each, so that every variable at each level is tested with all other variables at each of their levels. 2. Randomize sequence of testing. 3. Perform "anova" with rank order tests of significance.

Table 19. (continued).

B vs. C	1. Evaluate superiority of Method B over Method C when problem is easy to find. 2. Validate conclusions from variables search and full factorial experiments.	1. Select predetermined levels of risk (or confidence) and statistical power. 2. Run tests. 3. Rank order B and C units in terms of desired outputs. 4. Calculate $\bar{x}$ for B and for C units. 5. If B units outrank C units and if separation between their means is sufficient on power curve, superiority of B is established. 6. Even if there is no difference between B and C, B can be chosen if more economical.

Variables Search—the Rolls Royce of DOE Techniques

The systematic reduction of variation, as shown in Figure 8, starts with a multi-vari chart, whose purpose is to reduce a very large number of unrelated causes into a smaller family of related causes, generally 5 to 15. Variables search is the next step. Its objective is to pinpoint the Red X and, sometimes, one to three more interacting variables. Its methodology is simple.

Stage One

(1) The DOE team lists the most important input variables, A, B, C, D, E, F, G, H, and so on, in descending order of magnitude, that are likely to affect the output. (This is only a judgment call).

(2) Each input variable is next assigned two levels—a best (B), that is most likely to give good results, and a worst (W)—within the limits of reasonableness, that is likely to give poor results.

(3) Two experiments are then run, one with all variables at their best levels, the other with variables at worst levels. Two more experiments are run at the best and worst levels to assess experimental error. If the difference in outputs (D) between levels is greater than the difference in outputs within each level (as a result of the replication) by a factor of at least 5:1, the Red X is captured. If not, the right input variables were not chosen or the levels used may not have been the best or worst respectively and may have cancelled one another.

Stage Two

(1) The best level of the most important variable, A, is then combined with the worst levels of all the other variables. If A is important it will drag a desired output down. If not, it will not change the original output. If the output goes down partially or goes up even more than the original, A can be considered a possible Red X or Pink X or Pale Pink X, depending on the magnitude of the change, along with an interaction effect from another variable.

(2) The same component search "swap" is next performed, sequentially, on variables B, C, D, E, F, G, H, and so on. The unimportant variables that do not cause a reversal in outputs from Stage 1 are then considered for having their tolerances opened up for reduced costs. (Quite often, the cost reductions resulting from improved quality following a variables search experiment are matched by the cost reductions of larger tolerances.)

(3) Generally, one variable will be the dominant factor, the Red X. Sometimes, there are two or three more variables that are also important and could interact with one another. All of these important variables should be included next, in a "capping run," or validation experiment, at their best levels and with the unimportant variables at their worst levels. If the output is still at a desired high level, there is confirmation that the selected variables are truly important. This is further confirmed by selecting the worst levels of the important variables and the best levels of the unimportant variables in a final experiment. If the output is low, the confirmation is replicated.

Table 20 is an excellent example of a variables search experiment that was performed in response to a persistent quality problem in pilot run production. (It should have been conducted at the prototype stage of design). It took a technician no more than two days to run the experiment and another three days to optimize the input variables (not shown). It resulted in a savings of over $450,000.

To summarize, variables search has:

1. *Simplicity*. The methodology is simple and can be performed by technicians, with little statistical knowledge.
2. *Economy of experimentation*. The total number of experiments needed for Stage 1 is 4. For Stage 2, the number is 2n, where n is the number of variables being considered (for 10

Table 20. Variables search experiment.

Objective: *To optimize values and tolerances in order to improve quality and yields and to reduce material costs.*

Product: *Electronic engine control.*

Output Characteristics: *Idle speed current.*

Specifications: *650 M.A. to 800 M.A.*

7 components were selected by engineering as critical in descending order of importance

Factor Code	*Factor Description*	*Factor Value*	*Factor Tolerance*	*Factor Level Best (B)*	*Worst (W)*
A	Resistor: R 85	0.68 ohms	+ 5%	0.68 ohms	0.65 ohms
B	Pwr. sup. Volt. VCC	5.0 volts	± 5%	5.0 volts	4.75 volts
C	Resistor: R 77	100 ohms	± 1%	100 ohms	99 ohms
D	Resistor: R75	787 ohms	± 1%	787 ohms	779 ohms
E	Xsistor: Q 8 Saturat. Voltage	75 M.V.	150 M.V. Max.	75 M.V.	150 M.V.
F	Resistor R 79	43 ohms	± 5%	43 ohms	40.85 ohms
G	Integrated Circuit IC 4: off. Set volt.	0 M.V.	± 8 M.V.	0 M.V.	-8 M.V.

variables, the total is 20). For the capping run, the number is 2. The Taguchi orthogonal arrays require 4 to 15 times the number of experiments for comparative variables.

Variables search can be considered as a multidimensional model, where every corner of such a complicated structure is touched. In other words, every variable is tested with both levels of all other variables. Hence, all interaction effects are considered.

Table 20 (continued). Variables search experiment.

One unit was run with all the factors at the "best" (nominal or target) levels. The unit was then rerun with all the factors at the "worst" (tolerance limit) levels. The "best" and "worst" levels were then repeated. The results on the output (mole speed current) were:

Stage 1.	*Best level*	*Worst level*
	742 M.A.	*1053 M.A.*
	738 M.A.	*1050 M.A.*

A component search was then conducted to determine the effect of each factor on the output. The results were: the symbols R_B and R_W mean that the rest of the factors were maintained at the best levels and the worst levels, respectively.

Stage 2.	*Test No.*	*Combination*	*Results*
	1	A_W R_B	768 M.A.
	2	A_B R_W	1020 M.A.
	3	B_W R_B	704 M.A.
	4	B_B R_W	1051 M.A.
	5	C_W R_B	733 M.A.
	6	C_B R_W	1028 M.A.
	7	D_W R_B	745 M.A.
	8	D_B R_W	1018 M.A.
	9	E_W R_B	726 M.A.
	10	E_B R_W	1022 M.A.
	11	F_W R_B	733 M.A.
	12	F_B R_W	1020 M.A.
	13	G_W R_B	1031 M.A.
	14	G_B R_W	718 M.A.

Conclusions:

1. None of the component tolerances were critical or important, with the exception of the last—1C offset voltage—*the Red X*
2. The tolerances on six of the seven components can be opened up and the costs reduced.
3. The IC offset voltage tolerance needs tightening. Supplier Cp_Ks indicate excellent process capability.

SPC Tools: The Tail That Has Been Wagging the Dog

It is only when the diagnostic tools have reduced variability in both product and process at the design stage that SPC can be considered, and then, *only as a maintenance tool* to assure reduced variability in ongoing production. Yet, if a poll were taken in American industry among those companies that have attempted variation reduction, 90 percent would start with SPC, a clear case of the SPC tail wagging the DOE dog. And 90 percent of *them* would equate SPC with little more than control charts.

Table 21 lists four SPC tools, their objectives and methodologies. Positrol is especially important. *We have yet to learn that no process can really be controlled by looking at the product it produces.* That is too late. Key process variables must themselves be controlled, if the process is not to add to product quality woes. Similarly, process certification, which investigates all peripheral quality practices before the fact, is a fine example of prevention quality. Control charts, if used at all, should be the last installation in SPC.

Control Charts vs. Pre-Control: Horse and Buggy vs. the Jet Age

The control chart is yesteryear's technology. When developed by Dr. Walter Shewhart 60 years ago, it was a useful technique. Today, however, quality professionals should give up their attachment to this horse-and-buggy relic in favor of precontrol, which is simpler, less costly, more versatile, and statistically more powerful. Unfortunately, several OEM customers, especially some of the automotive companies, demand the use of control charts as a passport to their business. They force control charts down the throats of unknowing and unwilling suppliers, and they bludgeon into submission those knowledgeable suppliers who dare to point out that the control chart emperor wears no clothes!

Since control charts are widely known, they will not be explained beyond the short methodology described in Table 21. On the other hand, precontrol is only now coming into the consciousness of quality practitioners and needs a more detailed treatment.

Table 21. Four SPC. tools.

Tool	*Objective*	*Brief Methodology*
Positrol	Control and monitor process variables, identified as keys, thru variables search or full factorials.	1. Indentify the "who, how, where & when" key process parameters that can affect product made from the process; these will be monitored (positrol plan). 2. Establish a positrol log to record key process readings determined in positrol plan. 3. Later, convert positrol log into precontrol.
Process verification	Certify that all peripheral causes for poor quality at a workstation arc prevented.	1. Draw up a checklist of peripheral causes of poor quality (safety, environment, calibration, layout, goals, change notices, instructions, etc.). 2. Establish a team (process engr., development engr., quality engr., foreman, etc.,), to visit workstation & certify. 3. Periodically recertify.

Precontrol was invented in order to overcome the ills of control charts. Its rules are simple:

1. Divide the specification width by 4. The boundaries of the middle half then become the precontrol lines (i.e., the central half of the specification tolerance.) The area between these precontrol (PC) lines is called the green zone. The two areas between each precontrol line and each specification limit are called the yellow zones. The two

Table 21. (continued).

Tool	*Objective*	*Brief Methodology*
Control charts—$\overline{X}$ & $\overline{R}$ (Concepts similar for $\overline{P}$ & $\overline{C}$ charts)	To monitor & maintain reduced product/process variation, established with diagnostic tools (Table 19).	1. Take periodic subgroups (samples) of 4 or 5 units from process. A minimum of 20-30 times. 2. Calculate $\overline{X}$, R for each subgroup; also grand average, $\overline{\overline{X}}$, average range $\overline{R}$, upper & lower control limits (UCL & LCL). 3. Plot subgroup $\overline{X}$s & Rs vs. time. Draw in $\overline{\overline{X}}$ & UCL_X & LCL_X on $\overline{X}$ chart & $\overline{R}$, UCL_R & LCL_R on R chart. These become trial control limits. If a subgroup $\overline{X}$ or R falls outside control limits stop process; if not, start production. 4. Continue periodic sampling of process, maintain charts & periodically recalibrate control limits.
Precontrol	Same as control charts.	See test for detailed treatment. Precontrol is simpler, less costly, more statistically powerful than control charts.

areas beyond the specification limits are called the red zones. (See Figure 9.)

2. Before the start of production, take a sample of 5 consecutive units from the process. If all 5 fall within the green zone, the process is

Figure 9. The simplicity of precontrol.

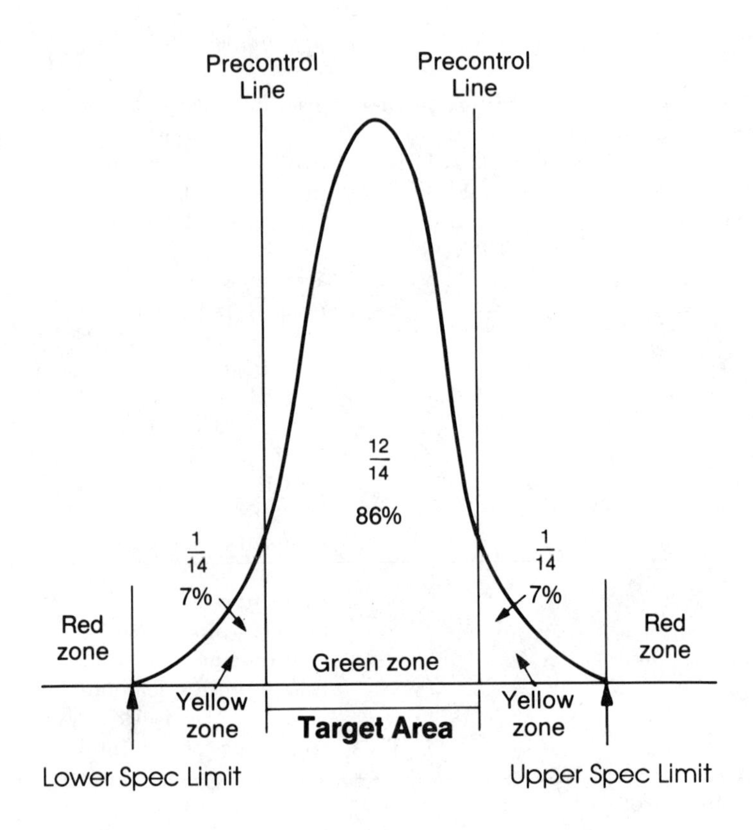

in control. Not even Cp_K calculations are needed. If even one of these units falls outside the green zone, determine the cause of the variation using the diagnostic tools of Figure 8 and Table 19 and correct the process.

3. Once production starts, take 2 consecutive units from the process periodically.

- If both units fall in the green zone or one unit is in the green and the other in one of the yellow zones, the process is in control. Continue production.

Table 22. The advantages of pre-control over control charts.

Characteristic	*Control Charts*	*Precontrol Charts*
1. Simplicity	**Complex*—Calculations of control limits involve formulas.	**Simple*—Precontrol lines are middle half of spec. width.
2. Use by operator	**Difficult*—Charting mandatory, interpretation unclear.	**Easy*—Green and yellow zones. A practical approach for all workers.
3. Mathematical calculations	**Involved*—$\bar{x}$, R, control limits and process limits must be calculated.	**Elementary*—Must only know how to divide by 4.
4. Small production runs	*Useless for production runs below 500 units. Sampling of 80-150 units before even trial limits can be established.	*Can be used for production runs above 20 units. Precontrol lines predetermined by specs. (which can be narrowed).
5. Recalculation of control limits	**Frequent*—No such thing in industry as a constant cause system.	**None needed,* unless specs. "goal posts" are moved inward.
6. Machine adjustments	**Time consuming*—Any adjustment requires another trial run of 80-150 units.	**Instant*—Based on 2 units.
7. Frequency of sampling	**Vague, arbitrary.*	**Simple rule:* 6 samplings between 2 stoppages/adjustments.
8. Discriminating power	**Weak*—Alpha risk of rejection by chart when there are no rejects is high.	**Excellent*—Alpha risk of rejection by precontrol is low—Less than 2% under worst conditions: Zero with C_{PK} of 1.66

Table 22: (Continued). The advantages of pre-control over control charts.

Characteristic	*Control Charts*	*Precontrol Charts*
	Beta risk of acceptance by chart (in control) when there are rejects is high. *Little relationship to specs.	Beta risk of acceptance by precontrol is low—Less than 1.36% under worst conditions. Zero with C_{PK} of 1.66
9. Attribute charts	$\bar{p}$, $\bar{c}$ charts do not distinguish between defect mode types or importance.	Attribute charts can be converted to precontrol charts by weighting defect modes and an arbitrary rating scale.
10. Economy	Expensive—Calculations, paperwork, larger samples, more frequent sampling, long trial runs.	Inexpensive—calculations simple, min. paperwork, small samples, infrequent sampling if quality is good. Process capability determined by just 5 units.

- If both units fall in the yellow zones, or even if one unit falls in the red zones, the process is out of control and requires stoppage for diagnosis.
- The process, after correction, will require a return to five units falling within the green zone before production can resume.
- The frequency of sampling two consecutive units is determined by dividing the time period between two stoppages by six.

The simplicity of precontrol is now obvious. Even the least sophisticated line or machine operator can use it and, more important, can make quick adjustments to assure defect-free production on thousands of units. The statistical power of precontrol, both in terms of Alpha (α) and Beta (β) risks, is superb, especially if processes have been previously scrubbed to achieve C_{PK}s of at least 1.33. While there is no need for charting in precontrol, plots of the two unit samples versus time can be maintained as a record. From such plots, C_{PK}s or frequency distributions can be derived easily. Finally precontrol can be used for: one-sided tightened specifications (relative to customer specifications); attributes, by converting attributes to variables on a 1 to 10 type arbitrary scale.

Because of ignorance of the weaknesses associated with control charts and because of the novelty of precontrol, Table 22 has been prepared to contrast the two SPC disciplines on a number of important characteristics.

SUPPLIER EVALUATION: WHY NOT THE BEST?

The purpose of supplier evaluation is to select the one or two very best suppliers of a commodity or part number from the available pool. A steering committee, drawn from upper management ranks, provides general guidance while the actual evaluations are made by interdisciplinary teams with representatives from purchasing, engineering, quality assurance and other functions, as needed. There are usually several such teams—one for each broad commodity, for example, plastics, die-casting, metal forming, semiconductors, chemicals, food, etc.

Each team draws up a list of suppliers, selected on the basis of ratings (see below), reputation, geographic location, size, and willingness to enter into a partnership relationship. A preliminary questionnaire, similar to that shown in the Appendix, is drawn up by the team and sent out to the list of suppliers. The responses from each supplier are evaluated by the team and two or three suppliers are then selected as the finalists for team visits.

During the team visits, the supplier's management is interviewed using an evaluation form similar to that in the Appendix. At the outset of these interviews, the team must clearly state that further interviews will be conducted with lower levels within the supplier's organization. The reason for the latter interviews is to separate "propaganda" answers from reality. The staff of such departments as engineering, purchasing, quality assurance and manufacturing usually provide frank insights into the real workings of the company.

After assessing the responses from each interview, the team members rate the finalist using a score ranging from 1 to 10. Later, the individual scores are compared and a final team score is prepared, which should be transmitted to all the finalists, along with an explanation of why they were chosen or not chosen as the top supplier.

A short explanation of the Appendix questionnaire is in order. It contains ten evaluation categories:

1. Financial strength, or experience.
2. Management commitment to excellence.
3. Design/technology strength.
4. Quality capability.
5. Cost competitiveness.
6. Service/flexibility.
7. Manufacturing skills.
8. Cycle-time concentration.
9. Employee participative climate.
10. Partnership extension to subsuppliers.

A customer company can choose categories other than the 10 described above, or assign different weights to each category, based upon what it considers important. Likewise, the detailed questions in each category can also be modified, with different weights attached to each question. The Appendix does have a certain symmetry with 10 categories and 10 questions in each category, so that the maximum score can add up to 1,000. Further, the questions are "tough"—almost of benchmark caliber. The object is to have high standards and strive for continuous improvement in supplier performance.

Supplier Quality Evaluation—Beyond the Trivia of Current Practices

The Appendix represents an overall evaluation of a supplier, assessing its management, technology, cost, quality, cycle time, and the like. Given the preeminence of quality, however, there is a need to assess a supplier's quality effectiveness in depth. Part II of the Appendix is an example of a "reach-out" evaluation. It too is divided into 10 quality categories or sybsystems with 10 questions in each category. As in Part I, the categories and the questions can be modified or given different weights, depending upon the importance that a customer company attaches to each topic.

Most quality evaluations of suppliers by customer companies deal with trivia—quality manuals, incoming inspection, sampling plans, data collection, the handling of rejects, and the like. The emphasis is on organization, documentation, and traditional quality control, which is obsolete. They do not deal with process control or quality training or teamwork or the parameters of the quality revolution. Companies, both large and small, copy these quality evaluations from one another in boiler-plate fashion. No wonder, then, that supplier quality performance is mediocre. The purpose of the Appendix, Part II, is to establish world-class quality standards. As stated throughout this briefing, both Part I and Part II can be used not only for supplier companies but also for customer companies as well. Customer companies must become the role model.

Supplier Qualification—Joining Hands

After the supplier is evaluated and selected through the above processes, the customer and supplier join forces to institute a formal supplier qualification program. The supplier should provide:

- Physical samples per agreed-upon specifications
- Test data on key parameters highlighted in such specifications (classification of characteristics)
- Reliability and stress-test data
- SPC data (C_{P_K} and pre-control charts) on the key parameters

The customer company can then conduct its own qualification of the supplier's physical samples. Generally, this is performed by an engineering group and includes:

- Parametric tests—to compare with the supplier's test data
- Reliability stress tests—to compare with similar supplier stress tests
- Destructive physical analysis (DPA)—where the supplier's samples are torn apart, dissected, x-rayed, and otherwise measured and analyzed to observe latent defects that may not be detected in conventional testing.
- Feedback to the supplier of the results of qualification

Table 23. Three alternatives in supplier rating

Alternative 1:	*No rating*
Pros:	• Numerical score, for vastly different suppliers, meaningless. • Supplier-customer interface should be based on supplier's actual performance. • Partnership implies constant communications and improvement.
Cons:	• No comparisons, esp. for suppliers of like commodities. • No ready reference for future procurements.
Alternative 2:	*Quality rating only*
Method:	1. Total cost of supplier's part: (Price + Cost of poor quality/delivery.) 2. % of lots accepted. 3. % value (or no.) of lots returned 4. % defective in samples tested.
Pros:	1. Other parameters of supplier performance—e.g., dependability, flexibility, service & cycle time are subjective & difficult to quantify. 2. Quality is the most important measure of supplier performance.
Cons:	1. To ignore other parameters is unfair & inaccurate. 2. Does not provide a total guide to future procurements. 3. Difficult to obtain failure costs. 4. Long lapse time in gathering field failure costs.

Qualification cycle time—one of the principal bottlenecks in new product introduction—can be drastically reduced from a typical 16 weeks (including life tests) to two weeks or less. This is done by transferring qualification responsibility to the supplier, with the customer monitoring the supplier's processes and tests. However, the customer must first trust the supplier and involve the supplier early in the design stage.

Supplier Rating—Pros and Cons

The rating of suppliers comes at the end of a long road of evaluation, qualification, and ongoing experience with supplier performance. It is a favorite topic of debate, especially among quality professionals. In general, there are three alternatives to supplier rating (see Table 23):

Table 23 (continued)

Alternative 3: All elements of supplier performance
Method:

Rating Element	*Basis of Score*	*Max. Points*
Quality	*Total cost* • Cost of incoming inspection + screening tests on line • Failure cost: field, line, rej./rework in incoming inspection • Cost of material delivered early (inventory) • Cost of wrong counts (+ or - from specified quantities)	35
Cycle time/delivery	• Total supplier cycle time • Supplier lead time • % items, or $, on time	30
Price leadership	Price vs. other suppliers in same commodity category	25
Service	• Responsiveness • Flexibility • Attitude • Technology • Documentation	10
	Max. Total	100

Pros: Complete, thorough, accurate, fair.

Cons: 1. Benefit/cost ratio may be low and may not justify the time and effort except for the most important suppliers.

1. No rating at all—the lowest cost approach and, perhaps, applicable only when the partnership is in an advanced stage of maturity.
2. Quality rating—used when the parameters of performance (other than quality) are subjective. Such parameters may include dependability, flexibility, cooperativeness, and cost. If the cost method of quantifying quality is selected, then it is paramount that the customer gather internal quality failure costs and external failure costs.

3. Rating based on all elements of supplier performance—this is the most rigorous approach, and also the most costly. It is the best approach if it is limited to the most important or the most troublesome purchase items, or where a decision must be made between two almost equal suppliers.

THE MARCH TO SELF-CERTIFICATION

Perfect quality, with zero defects from suppliers and no incoming inspection for customers, is the holy grail for many in this country. What they want is a practical method to reduce defects from the current 1 percent AQL* level to 100 parts per million (p.p.m.) or less. The following is a step-by-step roadmap to guide suppliers from unacceptably high defect levels to the joint bliss of zero defects and supplier self-certification:

A. Clear, firm, meaningful, and mutually acceptable specifications
B. Verification of the adequacy of the customer's design
C. Test equipment correlation between supplier and customer
D. Communications to the supplier's top management
E. Demonstration project at supplier's facility to resolve chronic quality problems
F. Supplier training for general management, technical staff, and other employees—in quality, SPC, cycle time management, and participative culture
G. Supplier workshop projects such as SPC, design of experiments, and JIT
H. Temporary extension of incoming inspection and standard sampling plans
I. Shainin lot plot plans and skip lot
J. Full certification and confident supplier self-certification

Each of these steps needs further explanation.

*AQL—Acceptable Quality Level. The statistical meaning of a 1 percent AQL is that if a supplier lot came in at exactly a 1 percent defect level, the probability of accepting that lot through a sampling plan would be 95 percent.

Clear, Firm, Meaningful, and Mutually Acceptable Specifications

At least half or even more of the quality problems between customer and supplier are caused by *poor specifications,* for which the customer company is largely responsible. Most specifications are vague or arbitrary. They are generally determined unilaterally by engineering, which lifts them from some boiler-plate document and embellishes them with factors of safety in order to protect its hide. When bids go out to suppliers, the latter are seldom consulted on specifications, and most suppliers are afraid to challenge specifications for fear of losing the bid.

In a partnership, these concerns evaporate. The supplier—since he is a partner—has already been selected and is involved early in the design stage. He is no longer afraid to share ideas with the customer's engineers. Cost, quality, and delivery targets are established and important parameters identified. The result: clear and firm specifications that are fair and meaningful and mutually acceptable to both parties.

So—the first cure for poor supplier quality is to eliminate the tyranny of capricious specifications. The quality engineer must meet with the supplier and development engineer and together review the specifications that have been difficult to meet. (The technique of realistic tolerances using scatter plots is a powerful tool in determining the correct value and tolerances of key input parameters. At this stage, the technique of "classification of characteristics" (described earlier) can draw the supplier's attention to certain "core" characteristics in the specifications rather than to the merely desirable or fuller requirements.

Verification of the Adequacy of the Customer's Design

Quite apart from the specifications themselves, there is always a possibility that inadequate design is the root cause of a quality problem. For example, it may be unfair to ask the supplier to turn a customer's "sow's ear design" into a silk purse. The customer can avoid imposing too many controls upon the supplier by increasing the margin of safety on the part or product. This may result in a slightly higher purchase price, but the overall cost will be lower.

Test Equipment Correlation

Often a quality problem results from differences in test methods and equipment, which lead to divergent readings between supplier and customer. A correlation program can prevent needless rejections, especially on parameters where measurements are difficult. In addition, instrumentation should be at least 5 to 10 times more accurate than that of the measured product parameter.

Communication to the Supplier's Top Management

This is a simple, but often overlooked step. There may be communication between two organizations at the lower levels—say customer quality assurance to supplier engineering, and customer purchasing to supplier sales. However, a quality problem may go forever unresolved if the supplier's senior management is kept unaware of or uninvolved in the problem.

Only when the four previous steps have been sufficiently investigated and there is little doubt that the supplier is primarily responsible for the quality problem should the customer proceed to the next step.

Demonstration Project at the Supplier's Facility

If a chronic quality problem has failed to respond to routine corrective action requests (CARs), a sure-fire solution is for the customer's engineers and quality assurance people to visit the supplier and immerse themselves in the problem. The investigation may be conducted jointly or the customer's team may take over completely, depending upon expertise and time availability. Statistical designs of experiments are powerful tools to unlock the secrets of problems where conventional engineering judgments have failed. Actually demonstrating the power of such experiments to the supplier may be the most effective way to make converts out of skeptics and foot-draggers.

Table 24. Supplier training: content and sequence.

Personnel	*Duration*	*Content*
General manager and staff	1-day seminar	Partnership; economics of quality; Quality management; SPC and design of experiments (DOE) overview; JIT overview; participative culture.
Technical personnel	2-day seminar	Quality system; disciplines in new product and process introduction; SPC and DOE (including relevant case studies).
Purchasing, engineers, QA and sub-suppliers	1-day seminar	Supply management; focus on quality, cost, and cycle time improvement.
Top, middle, and lower management	1-day seminar	Motivation principles; imperatives of a participative culture; job redesign; continuous process improvement, gain sharing (cleared in advance with supplier manager).

One of the requirements of a partnership is that the customer train supplier personnel. Table 24 is a suggested scope and sequence for the supplier's organization.

Supplier Workshop Projects

A seminar is merely a learning-by-listening exposure—a relatively ineffective tool for instruction retention. It should be followed by a workshop—with learning by *doing*. Make arrangements in advance with the supplier's management—preferably during the seminars—to select projects for workshops, where SPC, DOE, and JIT tools can be practiced. Establish project teams and have them coached by champions within the supplier's organization.

At a final workshop session, spokesmen for each team present their objective, the methods used to solve the problem, and the results achieved. The customer's trainer can then critique, counsel, and guide the teams toward optimum results. The members of the other teams benefit by examples relevant to them.

Temporary Extension of Incoming Inspection and Standard Sampling Plans

Steps A through G provide excellent opportunities for the supplier to improve his quality. But that improvement must be verified by traditional inspection sampling at the customer's site, until the customer is confident of the supplier's ability to control quality.

It is beyond the scope of this briefing to discuss the merits and demerits of most sampling plans. AQL sampling, like Mil-Std. 105 D, gives poor protection (Beta risk) to the consumer against poor supplier quality much worse than a specified AQL. LTPD, on the other hand, gives poor protection (Alpha risk) to the supplier against customer rejection of supplier quality better than desired. Given the world-wide drive toward zero defects, a defect level below 500 parts per million (i.e. 0.05% defective) is becoming the standard. The sooner both customer and supplier get away from these sampling plans and move toward certification, the better.

Shainin Lot Plot Plans and Skip Lot

There is only one sampling plan that can confirm defect levels below 500 ppm without the necessity of 100 percent inspection. This is the "lot plot plan" developed by the great Dorian Shainin. It is a variables plan (as opposed to an attribute plan), and the sample size is

Table 25. Application of Shainin lot plot plan to detect defects as low as 0.002 ppm.

Process Limits of $x \pm 5$ *within spec. limits*	*Max. Defect Levels in %/PPM (for 2-sided spec.)*
y = 1 : i.e., $\bar{x} \pm 1$	31.8% or 318,000 PPM
y = 2 : i.e., $\bar{x} \pm 2$	4.56% or 45,600 PPM
y = 3 : i.e., $x \pm 3$	0.26% or 2,600 PPM
y = 4 : i.e., $\bar{x} \pm 4$	0.012% or 120 PPM
	0.6
y = 5 : i.e., $\bar{x} \pm 5$	0.00006% or ++ PPM
y = 6 : i.e., $\bar{x} \pm 6$	0.0000002% or 0.002 PPM or 2000 parts per billion (PPB)

always 50 units, regardless of the size of the lot. First, the average and the standard deviation ($\bar{o}$) of the 50 units are calculated. Assuming a near-normal distribution, the process limits are then calculated and compared against the specification limits. Finally, the maximum defect levels are estimated using Table 25.

If process limits of $\bar{x} + y \times \bar{o}$ are within specification limits, the table can give the maximum defect levels possible for values of y from 1 to 6.

The Shainin lot plot plan can estimate defect levels much lower than 1 ppm—even those in the PPB range.

When inspection records on the supplier's quality performance show substantial improvement, the next step is skip lot, where only a fraction, usually 1/5 or 1/10, of the received lots are inspected. Skip lot is somewhat similar to a continuous sampling plan, with the difference being that it is used for lots received rather than for continuous production.

Full Certification and Supplier Self-Certification

As confidence in the supplier's quality builds through skip lot sampling, and as the customer approaches a near zero defect level in his production lines and in the field, the supplier achieves the status of full certification (but only on a part-number-by-part-number basis).

From that point forward, the emphasis shifts from external customer inspection to internal supplier outgoing inspection and, soon thereafter, from outgoing inspection and quality audits to total process control, as measured by precontrol. The customer, then, examines precontrol records and periodically monitors the supplier's processes. The supplier has now attained the status of self-certification.

Suppliers must be warned, however, that any slippage in quality performance can result in various penalties, ranging from the acceptance of rework and resorting costs to outright disqualification. There is no legal justification for a supplier to wash his hands of his financial responsibility simply because the customer has chosen not to check his product in incoming inspection.

4

Reducing Supply Costs

Improving supplier quality automatically means reducing supplier costs. While some percentage of this cost reduction must necessarily remain with the supplier in order to improve his profits, there must also be a reduction in the price to the customer company—in short, a win-win situation for both.

Besides quality improvement, there are several effective ways to achieve yearly reductions in supply costs of 10 percent and more:

- Cost targeting—mutual goals to beat the competition
- Early supplier involvement, "Sashimi" style
- Experience curves to gauge productivity improvements
- Group technology and part number reduction
- Specifications and "specmanship"
- Value engineering—an indispensable discipline
- Idea incentives for utilizing a supplier's brain, rather than his brawn
- Financial incentives/penalties for quality, delivery, and performance
- Inventory cost reduction (Chapter 5)
- Extension of all supply management techniques to sub-suppliers and sub-subsuppliers.

The purpose of cost targeting is to determine the difference between the estimated cost of a competitor's part or subassembly versus your own. Usually called "competitive analysis" or "reverse engineering," cost targeting is performed by professional, highly skilled cost estimators during the early stages of a product's design.

Once a benchmark cost is established, you are ready to set a target cost: a goal toward which your engineers strive to beat the competitor's cost, utilizing the partnership supplier as a member of the team. The result can be a spectacular cost reduction in the best spirit of true partnership.

EARLY SUPPLIER INVOLVEMENT—"SASHIMI" STYLE

Previous to the era of partnerships, designs were frozen before the bidding process. During bidding, most suppliers were reluctant to suggest cost reduction changes for fear of being considered deficient in their ability to meet requirements. After being selected, suppliers often rationalized that it was too late to submit any ideas for cost reduction. And if the supplier *did* submit an idea, the customer's engineer, feeling that his design was being challenged, might well reject it.

Within the framework of partnership, the climate can totally change and become conducive to cost reduction. Since the supplier has already been selected as a partner, he can get involved early in the design cycle and even in the conceptual stage. The designer and supplier now have a mutual goal: to beat the competitor's cost, following cost targeting. Ideas can now flow back and forth in a nonthreatening relationship.

Early supplier involvement has an even greater benefit: *a shortening of design cycle time.* This is one reason why new products from Japan enjoy a competitive advantage over new products introduced by the U.S. In fact, design cycle time may become one of the most important parameters of a company's long-term staying power. In Japan, engineers do not attempt revolutions in new design, as U.S. engineers are prone to do: At most, 25 to 50 percent of an older design is changed. Their engineers do not redesign by themselves or sequentially, with each step in series with the previous one. Instead, they farm out much of the subassembly design to their key suppliers, with work being done in parallel in order to save valuable design cycle time. The technique is called "sashimi"—reminiscent of the way

Japanese artistically arrange strips of sushi (raw fish), with each strip overlapping the next. Similarly, a supplier "overlapping" with the customer enables the Japanese to be working on the second- or even third-generation design, while U.S. engineers are struggling with a grandiose first-generation project.

EXPERIENCE CURVES TO GAUGE PRODUCTIVITY IMPROVEMENTS

Learning curves have long been used in industry to track reduced costs as a result of volume increases. An 80 percent learning curve means that for every doubling of unit volume, the unit cost becomes only 80 percent of the pre-doubled cost (in other words, a 20 percent cost reduction). Learning curves apply primarily to direct labor. Experience curves, which are based on the same principle, apply to total costs.

Every process has its own unique learning curve or experience curve. Information on these curves can be found in industrial literature. As an example, the generally accepted experience curve for the cost of integrated circuits (ICs) in the semiconductor industry is 70 percent. This translates into a 30 percent reduction that customers can expect for every doubling of IC volumes. A knowledgeable buyer, by having predetermined the experience curve for his product, can compare the supplier's prices with what should be a norm for that commodity. If the supplier's price is too high, either he is keeping a large part of the profit for himself or he is inefficient. A customer can use such insights during negotiations with suppliers.

Realize, however, that a doubling of the supplier's volume (here we mean total supplier volume, not just that volume shipped to a particular customer) is not directly related to a yearly volume. On new products, there may be a doubling of volume every two to six months. On established products, such doubling may not occur for 10 years or longer. Examples of the former abound in the dramatic way that prices of pocket calculators fell from over $300 in the early 1970s to the $5 to $10 range today. Similar experience curves now operate to reduce the prices of VCRs and computers. It is not inconceivable that, in a few years, the price of a full-fledged PC computer with peripherals will dip below $100!

GROUP TECHNOLOGY AND PART NUMBER REDUCTION

Chapter 2 detailed the economic advantage of a reduced supplier base. However, the cost leverage of a reduced supplier base can be crippled if the part number base is allowed to expand indiscriminately. Many companies are actually afflicted with a yearly rise in their new part number base.

As a first step in the prevention of this part number proliferation, a customer company must start with a reassessment of its strategic business units (SBUs). Table 26 is the well-known Boston Consulting Group (BCG) portfolio model for SBUs.

Table 26. B.C.G. Portfolio on value of business units in a corporation.

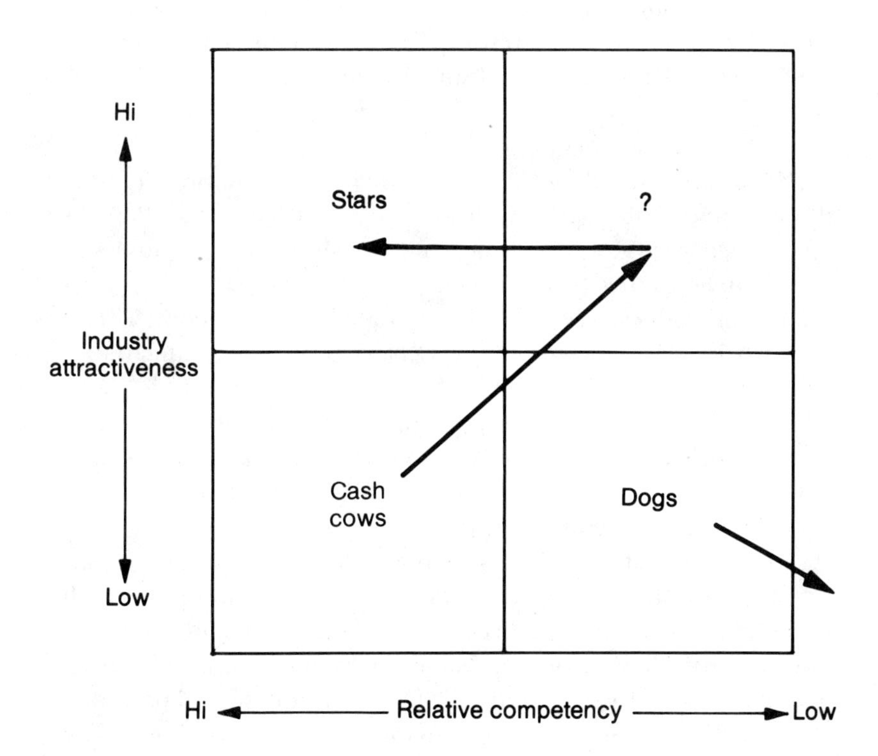

SBUs can be classified into four categories on the basis of their competency versus their industry attractiveness:

- "Star" SBUs: high competency and high industry attractiveness—should be the main focus of a company.
- "Question mark" SBUs: low competency and high industry attractiveness—should be nurtured with cash inflows to move them into the "star" category.
- "Cash cow" SBUs: high competency and low industry attractiveness—should be "harvested" to provide cash for the star and question mark SBUs.
- "Dog" SBUs: low competency and low industry attractiveness—should be divested.

The unprofitable, unattractive "dog" businesses form the starting point on the long road to part number reduction. Divestiture comes hard to most companies, but it is part of the concentration decision that Peter F. Drucker—the "dean of management"—advocates. A single, unprofitable divestiture can reduce a large volume of part numbers with one stroke.

Next in line should be the systematic reduction of product lines that are unprofitable or relatively unimportant to customers. Pareto's law, which indicates a nonlinear relationship between cause and effect, can be applied here. Generally, 80 percent or more of the total number of product lines contribute 20 percent or less to profit. Several product lines that constitute this 80 percent become candidates for elimination.

Thirdly, the same logic should apply to the vast array of models within a product line. Again, Pareto's 80:20 law can be applied to reduce those models that constitute 80 percent of the total but contribute 20 percent or less to profit.

Group technology is the last step in reducing an overgrown part number base. It is an operating management philosophy which recognizes that similarities occur in the design and manufacture of discrete parts. Similarities can be on the basis of shape, tolerances, manufacturing processes, and the like. As a result, several parts that appear to be different can be grouped together under a coding system, which can accurately describe any part, as opposed to the random choice of a part number. Unfortunately, instead of there being a single standard coding system, there are over 40 different ones, with 11 in the U.S. alone. But converting from a random part numbering system to a group technology system can result in enormous cost savings, as shown in Table 27.

To summarize, reducing the part number base starts with the elimination of "dog" businesses, followed by the elimination of unprofitable products and models, followed by the reduction of different part numbers through group technology.

Table 28 gives the most appropriate method for each reduction, along with the results that can be achieved in a two to three-year span. Eliminating single part number can save anyhere from $1300 to $12,000 depending on the accounting methods used.

Table 27. Cost savings potential from group technology.

52%	in	New part design
10%	in	No. of drawings
30%	in	New shop drawings
60%	in	Industrial engineering time
20%	in	Production floor shop space
42%	in	Raw material stocks
69%	in	Setup times
70%	in	Throughput times
62%	in	Work-in-process (WIP) inventory
52%	in	Overdue orders

Table 28. A systematic method to achieve part number and supplier reduction.

Area	*Method of Reduction*	*% Reduction*
Businesses	Portfolio analysis	25
Product lines	Pareto analysis	33
Models	Pareto analysis	50
Part nos.	Group technology	75
Suppliers	Partnership	90

SPECIFICATIONS AND SPECSMANSHIP

Specifications represent a gold mine for cost reductions. Most specifications are vague, arbitrary and poorly established. In general, the customer tends to overspecify them for the following reasons:

- Designer caution and/or pride of invention
- Management's desire to emulate a competitive feature, regardless of the value of the feature
- Eager salesmen promising the moon
- Customer unable to separate "must" specifications from merely desirable ones
- Government regulations
- Unreasonable pressures from society

But there are also reasons for inadequate specifications:

- Reliability is seldom a quantitative specification
- Customer's lack of knowledge of precise requirements
- Supplier's lack of knowledge of application and end-use
- Poor communication between customer and supplier

In order to convert this liability into an asset, the customer must change his entire approach to the formation of specifications:

- Involve the supplier early on in the formulation
- Scrutinize each parameter in the list for maximum value at minimum cost
- Pay attention to the supplier's suggestions for cost reduction and quality improvement, since he obviously is the expert at manufacturing his commodity.
- Review all parameters in the specification and classify the truly important ones with a minimum Cp_K of 1.33.

The end-result should be specifications that are fair, meaningful, challenging, complete, and cost effective.

VALUE ENGINEERING—AN INDISPENSABLE DISCIPLINE

Value engineering (VE), founded in the United States, has enormous benefits, and yet, incomprehensively, it remains little known and little used in the country of its origin. Japan, on the other hand, has adopted value engineering as a mandatory discipline, and it's easy to understand why if one considers all its benefits:

- An average reduction of 25 percent in procurement costs. A minimum 10 percent reduction can be achieved with little imagination.
- A 10:1 return on investment.
- Improved customer satisfaction—a higher value/price ratio.
- Improved quality/reliability.
- Serendipity in technology and materials.
- Higher employee morale through team-building.

Origin. VE started in the materials management function, when Larry Miles, in General Electric's purchasing research department, was asked to find substitutes for scarce materials during World War II. He discovered—perhaps through serendipity—that the substitute materials were not only less expensive but better in quality as well! Thus was born the discipline of value engineering.

The FAST (Function Analysis using a Systems Technique) diagram

In traditional cost reduction, the part or product is treated as a "given," whereas in VE, one examines the *function* that the product performs and then looks for alternative ways to provide that function at less cost and with better quality. These functions consist of two categories: (1) basic functions that make the product work; and (2) supporting functions that make the product sell. Supporting functions are further divided into four types:

- Assuring dependability.
- Assuring convenience.
- Satisfying the user.
- Attracting the user.

The highest order basic function is called the "task."

An important VE tool is the FAST diagram. (See Table 29: a FAST diagram for a spin cast fishing reel.) Start with the task on the left of the diagram and apply a "how and why" logic to the functions. For

Table 29. Function Analysis Systems Technique (FAST).

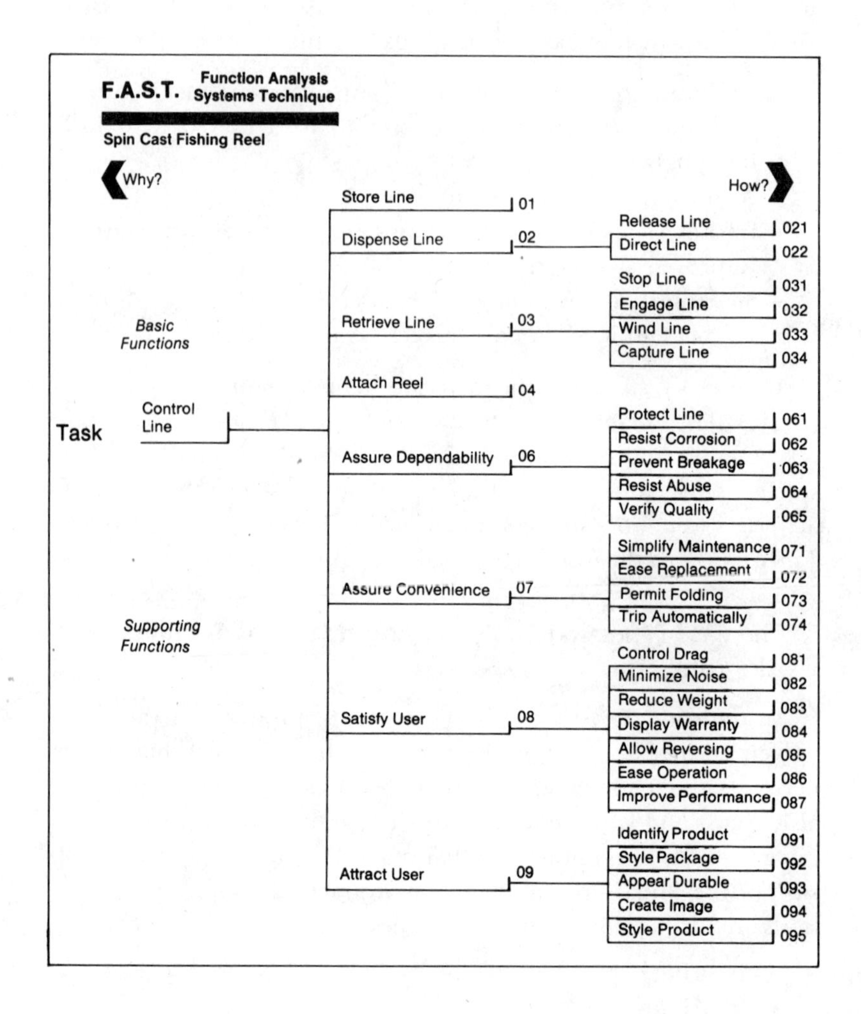

example, ask, "How do we perform the task?" Then examine the functions—both basic and supporting—that answer the question. Place your answers to the right of the task in the FAST diagram. Further "how" questions lead to the next order of functions and so on, until additional new questions can only be answered with the product's parts and/or manufacturing processes. A FAST diagram, being a function chart, should not include these parts or processes. Similarly, "why" questions (e.g., "Why do we perform a particular function?") lead from right to left in the function tree until the task is reached.

Cost Breakdown

The next step is to break down product costs, part by part, with each part further broken down into material, labor, and overhead costs. Parts have costs and parts have functions; therefore, functions have costs. Since a single part could perform multiple functions, a VE team systematically allocates the various detailed costs to each of the lowest order functions on the right side of the FAST diagram. This gives a precise picture of how the total cost of a product is distributed among the various functions that a product performs.

Value Research

Input from end-users/customers is the most important part of the VE process. Through surveys or meetings with end-users, the product's features and its faults are rated on a scale of one to ten. An end-user sample of 30 is sufficient to obtain a reasonable profile of customer satisfaction, dissatisfaction, or neutrality with respect to a product feature.

Value Equals Function Worth/Function Cost

These end-user ratings are then allocated to the furthest right functions in every branch of the FAST diagram, so that every function has a cost and an end-user worth. Functions analyzed in this fashion fall into four categories (Table 30).

Table 30. Function: cost analysis.

Function worth (end user)	Function cost	Action Required
High	Low	None (advertise)
High	High	Reduce cost
Low	Low	Attempt improvement of worth
Low	High	Attempt elimination of function

Creativity Phase of VE

Albert Einstein once said that "Imagination is much more important than knowledge." His spirit is captured in the next phase of VE—the creativity or brainstorming phase. The VE team conjures up alternative ideas—wild or sober—to satisfy the functions. In general, the *quality* of the final solution will be proportional to the *quantity* of ideas in the brainstorming phase.

Creative thinking is stimulated by a checklist. The following is a sample:

- Eliminate the part
- Simplify it
- Alter it to accommodate a high-speed method
- Use standard parts or materials
- Use lower cost materials
- Use lower cost processes
- Use a higher cost material that can simplify design and production
- Consider other methods of fabrication
- Increase quality/reliability with no cost increase
- Increase differentiation in order to fetch a higher price
- Consider features that are important to customers
- Strive for better service
- Increase dependability
- Provide greater flexibility
- Strive for earlier delivery

The next phases of VE are the evaluation phase, where the ideas are narrowed down to those with greatest value improvement potential, and the development phase, where feasible models are tested for maximum quality at maximum cost.

Value engineering is a particularly powerful tool in the materials management-supplier link. The engineer-purchasing-supplier team should put a dollar sign on every parameter, every tolerance, every finish and then, in Pareto law fashion, determine value engineering alternatives to all the high cost requirements. In a climate of partnership, the supplier can make suggestions for cost and quality improvements, whereas he would be reluctant to do so in the old adversarial relationship.

IDEA INCENTIVES—UTILIZING A SUPPLIER'S BRAIN, NOT HIS BRAWN

To elucidate this section, think about taking a part and sending it out for bids to two suppliers, A and B. Table 31 describes a few possible scenarios. In the first scenario, we assume that both suppliers quote per the established specification. With B's lower price, assuming that all other factors (such as quality and delivery) are the same, B gets the order.

In the second scenario, we assume that both suppliers turn in value engineering ideas to reduce cost. Supplier A turns in idea X, which is accepted by the customer's engineers, and his price is reduced to $0.90 per part. Supplier B does not bother to come up with any cost reduction ideas. By the rules of idea incentives, A gets the order.

In the third scenario, Supplier A turns in idea X and Supplier B turns in idea Y—one that is separate from idea X. Assume that both ideas are acceptable to the customer's engineers. If there is no time for further negotiations, B gets the order.

If, however, there is time and the incentive ground rules have been defined in advance, the customer can initiate another round of bidding, with B's idea given to A and vice versa. Both suppliers then requote. In this fourth scenario, B's price is still lower than A's. This poses a dilemma. If B gets the order because of lower price, A—in all likelihood—would feel that the rug was pulled out from under him.

With his idea stolen, he does not want to conduct any further business with the customer company. If the order is split between A and B, however, the price will be higher because of lower volumes. What, then, is the solution?

Ideally, the customer would give B the order, but pay both suppliers A and B a *royalty*—limited to the order or to a year's contract—for the use of their ideas. The customer saves at least $0.20 per part and can afford to give A and B each a 2 or 3 cents per unit royalty payment. B is happy to get the order as well as a royalty bonus. A is happy for parlaying his idea into cash.

The U.S. Department of Defense (DOD) provides the genesis for idea incentives. In recent years, DOD's image has been tarnished, but it has contributed many a management innovation to industry. In the 1950s, DOD would ask its defense contractors for cost reduction ideas. The latter obliged, but received nothing in return except a financially empty "thank you." The idea pipeline dried up faster than the trickle in the Sahara desert!

Robert McNamara, Defense Secretary under President Kennedy, saw that financial incentives to contractors stimulate the flow of ideas and, as a result, value engineering clauses were born. As a reward to the contractor, the total savings from his idea would be shared on an equitable basis between DOD and the contractor. In a follow-on contract, the contractor would receive a royalty payment, representing up to 20 percent of the total savings from his idea, even if that contractor did not end up as the successful bidder.

Table 31. A case study in idea incentives.

		Supplier A	Supplier B
Scenario 1	Unit price (per print)	$1.00	$0.95
Scenario 2	Unit price (idea X from Supplier A)	0.90	0.95
Scenario 3	Unit price (idea X from A idea Y from B)	0.90	0.85
Scenario 4	Unit price quotes from both A and B on ideas X and Y	0.80	0.75

It is, indeed, unfortunate that this use of idea incentives and royalty payments has not found its way into commercial industry. How long are we going to ask our suppliers, when checking in, to leave their brains outside?!

FINANCIAL INCENTIVES/PENALTIES FOR QUALITY, DELIVERY, AND PERFORMANCE

In addition to royalty payments, the Department of Defense has incentive contracts with its suppliers for quality, delivery, and performance. These contracts operate on the principle of the carrot and the stick—they reward better-than-agreed-upon quality, reliability, delivery, or performance but they penalize any failure to meet these targets. Both incentives and penalties are percentages—usually in the range of 5 to 10 percent—of the contract price.

However, this excellent principle of incentive contracting is almost unknown to commercial industry, except for the construction and housing sectors. Yet, there is no reason why customer and supplier companies cannot enter into such agreements in the normal course of business. Figure 10 represents various arrangements for incentives and penalties as applied to delivery, quality, reliability, and performance, respectively. The share line, which determines the degree of incentive or penalty, can be straight, curved, discontinuous, or a step function. In most applications, the share line is a straight line, with its slope determining the amount of incentive or penalty.

Incentive/penalty contracts should be invoked only under special circumstances:

1. If there is a repetitive problem between a customer and supplier company, either in the area of delivery, quality, reliability, or performance. (If the problem is delivery only, there is no need for an incentive/penalty contract for the other parameters.)
2. If the repetitive problem is measurable in dollars and is large enough so that an improvement can benefit both parties.
3. If the incentive/penalty contract applies when the freedom to change suppliers is limited, either because:

Figure 10. Supplier incentives/penalties.

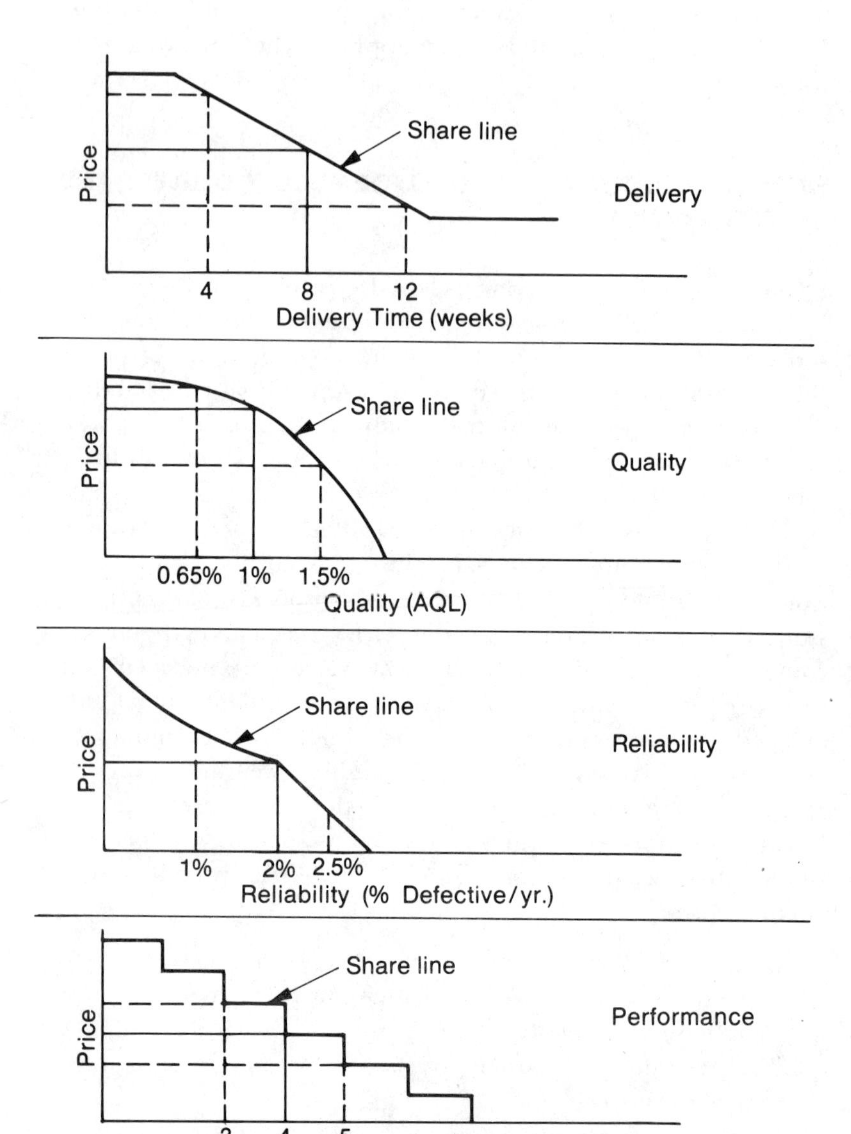

- the supplier has the best technology, price, or quality, but is deficient in one of the other parameters of performance that needs upgrading.
- the supplier is a sister division in a large company, which has an edict to buy internally.
- there is a partnership relationship with the supplier.

4. If the problem can be corrected through the incentive route.

Incentive contracting has not come of age in the commercial world, but with prior negotiations and agreement between customer and supplier, it can be a powerful tool for reducing quality costs, improving consumer value, and reducing supplier lead time and cycle time.

EXTENSION OF ALL SUPPLY MANAGEMENT TECHNIQUES TO SUBSUPPLIERS AND SUB-SUBSUPPLIERS

A major objective of this briefing is to improve supplier quality, cost, and delivery. But even if all the techniques described thus far are put into effect, the job will only be partially complete if it is confined to just the first-level supplier. A supplier is handcuffed in his overall improvement efforts if he does not pass on his techniques to his supplier, and that supplier to his supplier, and so on, through several such customer-supplier links.

The Japanese Shock Absorption Phenomenon. One of the best illustrations of this chain reaction is the Japanese strategy to combat the falling dollar and the rising yen in order to continue the export juggernaut. Let us assume that there is a 40 percent devaluation of the dollar vis-á-vis the yen. American manufacturers are lulled into complacency by predicting a 40 percent rise in the cost of Japanese goods landed in the U.S. The Japanese, however, go to their small supplier base and boldly ask for a 40 percent price decrease. The suppliers, in the spirit of partnership, contribute a small percentage—say 5 percent—to the price reduction by themselves. But the much larger contributions to reduction come from successive price reductions throughout the 10 to 14 links in the long and tightly knit

Japanese supply chain. Each subsupplier in the chain makes his small contribution to cost reduction, but the cumulative impact is amplified to reach the target level of a 40 percent cost reduction.

This unique "shock absorption" phenomenon in Japan is strengthened by two factors. First, the number of links in the supply chain, from raw materials to end consumer, is much larger in Japan—10 to 14 links versus 5 to 7 links in the U.S. Hence, there are more layers to absorb the shock of cost reduction. (The same technique is used to soften the impact of a recession.) Secondly, the links between various layers of suppliers is much stronger in Japan. Toyota, as an example, directly influences subsuppliers four levels down! In the U.S., on the contrary, we are just now at the dawn of a *one-level* partnership with our immediate suppliers. Vertical penetration of the supply chain must become a much higher priority with customer companies in the U.S. if we are to compete successfully in a global marketplace.

5

Inventory and Cycle Time Reduction

Inventory—From Asset to Liability. In corporate balance sheets, inventory is still considered an asset. However, in the era of the 1980s, inventory is looked upon as "the graveyard of poor management." The reason for the old thinking was simple. It never appeared on a P and L statement. Managers' performance was never evaluated on the basis of the inventories they carried.

But as the emphasis shifted from profit on sales to return on assets and investments, asset turns became an important part of the corporate calculus:

$$\text{Asset turns} = \frac{\text{sales}}{\text{total assets}} = \frac{\text{sales}}{\text{inventory + receivables + fixed assets}}$$

This means that return on assets can be measurably improved by reducing inventory, which traditionally accounts for 20 to 40 percent of total assets. Furthermore, reduced inventories help to improve cash flow management. This, in turn, makes a corporation less dependent on the tyranny of the stock analyst and the whims of a stock market.

INVENTORY IS THE RESULT; CYCLE TIME THE MEANS

Like profits, inventory is only a result, a measurement. Cycle time provides the means. Cycle time is the clock or calendar time spent from the start of a process to its completion—whether that process be a manufacturing cycle, a new design introduction, order processing, or any support function operation. Through effective cycle time management, cycle times can be reduced by factors of 10, 20, or even 50 times. Reduced cycle times mean lower inventories. Lower inventories translate into cost savings, at figures between 20 to 40 percent of average inventory dollars—again, both for suppliers and customers.

The phantom chasing of direct labor. Today, direct labor represents only a small percentage of the total manufacturing cycle time. Hence, the reduction of direct labor, long a management preoccupation, is no longer necessary. (Equally irrelevant is cost accounting that monitors and controls direct labor costs, but in the process spends more than the entire costs of direct labor!). This means that the U.S. quest for cheap labor abroad is an anachronistic exercise. Equally meaningless is the urge to automate, if the purpose is only to reduce direct labor.

The major elements of non-value-added cycle time—idle time, queue time, set-up time, storage time, and transport time—are responsible for most of the time wasted in manufacturing. For example, does it make any sense for a product to be partially built in the U.S., sent to one overseas location for final assembly, another overseas center for test, and then returned to the U.S. for a final quality audit and distribution? Transport cycle time is increased from hours to days, even weeks! Yet, U.S. industry is replete with this unbelievable, almost criminal, waste of precious cycle time. In one instance, a part crossed the oceans seven times before it reached its eventual customer!

THE RIVER ANALOGY

The river analogy can help attack and reduce inventory. Think of the volume of water in a river as inventory. This river volume has width, length, and depth. So does inventory. The width comes from product variety—a proliferation of models and parts needed to support a full line to customers. This means more inventory to accommodate product variety. The factory of the future, equipped with computer integrated manufacturing (C.I.M.) and other support mechanisms, can produce a product variety almost as economically as a narrow line—a distinct strategic advantage. But as an interim step toward this end, product variety must be reduced as inventory is reduced, along the lines discussed in Chapter 4.

A river has length. In inventory terms, length means cycle time. The next sections describe a systematic method to reduce cycle time. Finally, a river has depth. The analogy of rocks in the river suggests the different approaches to inventory control between the U.S. and Japan (see Figure 11). The U.S. approach is to avoid the rocks by raising the level of the water; i.e., increasing inventories to avoid quality problems, supplier delays, etc. The Japanese, on the other hand, deliberately reduce the level of the water in order to expose the

Figure 11. U.S. vs. Japanese approaches to inventory.

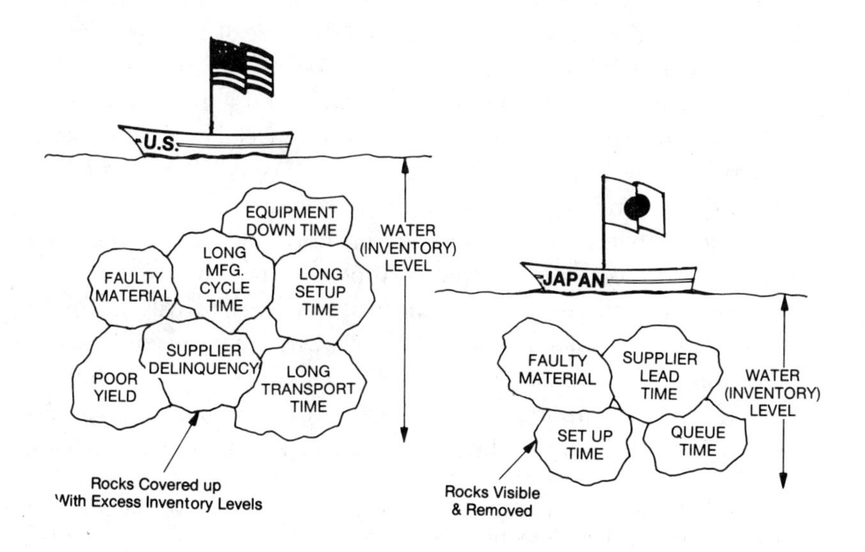

rocks and remove them. Lowering the level of inventory gives visibility to the several quality and delivery problems. Visibility, in turn, gives urgency to their resolution.

A SYSTEMATIC APPROACH TO CYCLE TIME REDUCTION*

Table 32 captures the anatomy of a powerful cycle time reduction system. The following section describes the five major attributes of the system, followed by five subtler nuances that enrich these attributes.

1. Structured Flow Paths

The focused factory. The conventional wisdom of yesterday was to build a wide variety of products within a single plant. This meant the nonspecialization of products and a lack of employee "ownership." In the focused factory, near-autonomous small factories (sometimes called plants within a plant) are dedicated to the exclusive production of a limited number of close-related products.

Product flows. The old order is also based on a process flow, where the product travels all over a plant because of process-centered islands in fragmented locations. As a result, transport time and waiting time escalate. In one factory, a part would actually travel nine miles within a plant area of 30,000 square feet before shipment! Structured flow paths, on the other hand, are based on a smooth product flow (preferably U-shaped for maximum operator flexibility and control) that drastically reduces transport time and waiting time. It does create some duplication of processes, but the costs of such duplication can be minimized if the process in each focused factory is made smaller, simpler, and more flexible, with small lots of product.

Support operations integration. The old order also has compartmentalized line support operations, where each support operation is centralized within one of the plant's bureaucratic islands, which are

*The author is greatly indebted to Dr. Ed Heard, President of E. Heard Associates and one of the national authorities on cycle time management, for the concepts and framework of the five attributes of cycle time reduction.

Table 32. The anatomy of cycle time reduction.

Attributes	*Nuances*				
	Autonomy	*Flexibility*	*Simplicity*	*Visibility*	*Urgency*
A. Structured flow paths					
B. Continuous flows					
C. Linear operations					
D. Dependable supply/demand					
E. People power					

connected only by vertical linkage to a far-removed boss. The results are the erection of departmental walls, battles over turf, and a lack of teamwork. In the structured flow path system, these centralized support operations are broken up (except for one or two specialists who can act as internal consultants) and its members assigned to focused factories. This combination of product flow and support operations dedicated to a focused factory is referred to as a *group technology cell.*

2. Continuous Flows

This attribute of cycle time management is quality control at its best. The object is to ensure that poor designs, defective materials, unstable processes, and marginal workmanship are not only corrected, but prevented from happening again, so that there is a continuous, uninterrupted flow of product with zero defects, 100 percent yield, minimal variation within specification, and no inspection and test. This, of course, is an ideal, but Chapter 3, with its powerful SPC and design of experiment tools, offers an excellent blueprint for the eventual attainment of this ideal.

3. Linear Operations

"Pull" vs. "push" product control. The fame of the Japanese Kanban system has heightened interest in the "pull" system of product control versus the old "push" system. In the latter, operators pile up product at a work station, regardless of the pile-up of inventory further down the line. In the pull system, the back end of the line paces the entire line, with each previous work station producing only the exact amount needed by the next station.

The advantage of small lots. A central feature of the pull system is the emphasis on small lots. This saves space, reduces the amount of rework required if a quality problem should arise, and gives maximum visibility to the problems because they stop the entire line. Finding an immediate and permanent solution therefore becomes an urgent priority. The greatest impact of small lots is the reduction of queue time on parts waiting to be processed.

Set-up time reduction. Small lots, however, require drastic reductions in set-up time in order to reduce cycle time. Through people power (see 5 below) and ingenious industrial engineering, you can reduce set-up times by factors of 60:1!

Constant output. The benefits of pull systems are limited if the total quantity required by master schedules is allowed to vary from day to day. Such schedules should have nearly constant rates—otherwise known as "fidelity" or "linearity." However, linearity does not mean only one model in a focused factory run at a given time. There can be model mixes, but the total output of the mix should be nearly constant. Radio terminology can be used to describe the concept of linearity. In FM, or frequency modulation we have varying frequency and constant amplitude. Linearity is like FM: The frequency or repetition rate of each model can vary, but the total amplitude or volume should remain constant.)

4. Dependable Supply and Demand

In order to get your suppliers and your customers to practice cycle time management, you must first convince them of its effectiveness. You must become the showcase. You can do this by reducing work-in-process (W.I.P.) cycle time and leaving somewhat larger inventories as buffers in raw materials and finished goods.

Customers become converts when you can deliver their orders in a much shorter time than previously—a decided advantage over competition, especially with the added advantages of higher quality and lower cost. The customer can then begin, with greater confidence, to order smaller quantities more frequently. In time, he can be persuaded to grant longer term contracts, rolling linear demand forecasts, and progressively frozen shipment schedules—in short, a partnership customer. Similarly, suppliers can be encouraged, especially within the framework of partnership, to deliver a linear output of their products in smaller, more frequent lots. But, as with many other practices, the company must be a role model to its partnership suppliers.

5. People Power

This attribute of cycle time management has been saved for last because it is the most important. This point is best illustrated by a story. When the Japanese suppliers to a large global manufacturing company visited their American counterparts, the Japanese delegation reported that they saw no great difference between their physical plants and the U.S. plants. The processes and equipment were also similar, as were the workers. But, the report went on, U.S. management was not utilizing the workers' minds. However, if they did—watch out, Japan!

Most U.S. managers know this people power instinctively, but they do little about it. There are sporadic attempts—worker-level quality circles, suggestion systems, Scanlon plans, some form of gainsharing. But real, full-throated worker participation has not come about because management is not truly involved with its workers, does not fully believe in their ability to solve problems, and does not want to relinquish vestiges of power. By contrast, Japanese managers in the U.S. have mobilized the same American workers into constructive, creative partners. What, then, can be done?

American management must:

- Cross-train its workers so that they can become multi-skilled.
- Remove rigid job classifications and reduce their number.
- Eliminate individual incentives and encourage team-building.
- Establish focused factories to nurture a sense of ownership by the team.
- Coach workers in simple problem-solving, as detailed in Chapter 3. Once trained and encouraged, workers often perform better than engineers. (There are far more problems than managers can solve by themselves. Think of what can happen with a whole factory turned loose on problem-solving.)
- Treat the next operation as a customer, the previous operation as a supplier; specify the requirements desired by the "customers" and measure progress against these requirements.
- Mingle with workers daily. Be visible. Be helpful. Act as coaches, not bosses.
- Eliminate fear among workers. It is corrosive and unbecoming

for a country that prides itself on being the world's foremost democracy.
- Redesign workers' jobs to make them less boring, more meaningful—every employee can be a manager in his or her own area.

THE FIVE NUANCES THAT ENRICH THE FIVE ATTRIBUTES OF CYCLE TIME MANAGEMENT

Table 32 is a matrix of the five attributes of cycle time management and the five associated nuances of these attributes. These nuances are:

- *Autonomy.* Autonomy is necessary to promote motivation and ownership among workers in a focused factory. It does not mean that there should be no management feedback and control. But employees should feel free to innovate, to "reach out," even to make mistakes.
- *Flexibility.* There should be flexibility within the focused factory to move stations and processes as needed. If you are realigning your manufacturing and process strategies, start flexible manufacturing systems (FMS), supported by computer integrated manufacturing (CIM), in order to take full advantage of these concepts in the factory of the future.
- *Simplicity*—is required in all operations. The best designs are the simple ones that can easily be put together. "Simplify before you automate" is the new watchword. Simpler processes are less likely to break down. Further, automation's goal should be to reduce cycle time and drudgery, not direct labor.
- *Visibility.* One of the main benefits of a "pull" or Kanban system in cycle time management is that problems of any type cause line shut-downs and become highly visible to management and workers alike.
- *Urgency.* Once the problem is visible, the solution becomes urgent. Since the entire focused factory is affected, the urgency generates team solutions, with experts and workers helping one another to achieve permanent answers.

The most frequently asked question about cycle time management is: "Where do we begin implementation?" As with other "processes" (as opposed to "programs") of importance, the start should be with top management exposure, education, and commitment. From that point forward, the following is a suggested roadmap:

1. *Performance measurement parameters* must shift the focus away from profit to return on investment (R.O.I.), from direct labor to manufacturing cycle time, and from forecasting to customer response time. Cycle time, in particular, is an amazing integrator of quality, cost, delivery, and effectiveness.

2. *Pilot selection for a focused factory:* Rather than immediately breaking up a large plant into several focused factories, a single focused factory should act as a pilot, representing a product family that is based on similar processing requirements and using similar standard components.

3. *A focused factory management team:* From a human relations viewpoint, this may be the hardest step, since it disrupts traditional functional organizations and cuts into "empires." A first step, therefore, may be assigning a task force role to a selected focused-factory management team. As the task force begins to operate and succeed, it can turn into a focused-factory organization, with an autonomous team consisting of a manager and members from every function within manufacturing, followed soon after by other supporting functions, such as sales, engineering, materials management, and quality assurance.

4. *People power.* A focused factory, with its small size, natural work units, client relationships, quick feedback of performance and sense of ownership, has a far greater chance of welding its people into a family and unleashing full people power. The Hawthorne effect may also come into play, as success becomes more widely recognized. Training of the workforce in multiple skills and problem solving should begin with creating the focused factory.

5. *Poor quality, the number one rock.* In the "rocks in the river" analogy, the rocks, or problems, raise the level of the water, or inventory, if they are not broken up. But there is no rock more formidable

than the rock of poor quality. Tackling all quality problems must be the highest priority in the focused factory—from product yields to processing times, from incoming inspection to supplier process control.

6. *Linear operations.* Only after the quality problems are solved or greatly reduced can you make your operation linear. This is done first through the use of standard containers, small lots, and set-up reduction, followed by near constant outputs, and finally, a pull system.

7. *Dependable supply and demand.* The last steps are influencing suppliers and customers. A demonstration of achievements in your own plant is worth a thousand words and is the best sales tool to request blanket contracts and smaller, more frequent deliveries to the customers and from the suppliers.

SHORT-TERM LEAD TIME REDUCTION

The cycle time management process detailed earlier is long-range in nature, spanning three to five years in the best of companies. But companies are in a hurry. What, then, can be done in the short-term, especially toward the reduction of supplier lead time? Supplier lead time (for initial procurement, before the pipe line is filled) can account for up to 80 percent of total cycle time, from customer order to shipment. Reducing supplier lead time requires a systematic approach, as outlined here. (Some of the points have been covered in detail earlier in this text and are merely summarized for emphasis.)

1) Enter into long-term contracts (2 years).
2) Make stable forecasts for a 12-month period, updated each month, with only gradual ramp-ups or ramp-downs.
3) Place blanket orders, using variable volume pricing.
4) Authorize a partial build, up to the longest cycle time in the supplier's production but with the least dollar expenditure (e.g., in semiconductors, the cycle time up to the wafer fabrication stage is over 80 percent of total cycle time, but only 40 percent of total cost), and make a commitment to buy material up to that point.

5) Offer financial incentives for lead time reductions (see Chapter 4).
6) Order electronically through paperless, instantaneous transactions.
7) Do a re-vamped analysis (Table 33), with a focus on small quantities and daily deliveries (some factories in Japan receive materials 24 times a day, delivered straight to production lines from supplier trucks) for maximum inventory turns and space reductions.
8) Practice local sourcing, where possible. Forcing suppliers to establish local warehouses simply to reduce customer inventory is, at its most charitable best, a band-aid that puts the entire burden of added inventory on the supplier, with the customer indirectly paying for it in the long run.
9) Ship by air (if the savings in lead time reduction exceed the transportation cost).
10) Assist the supplier (covered in Chapter 2).
11) Stay close to the supplier: Partnership does not work by remote control or through the writing of memos. It requires frequent visits to the supplier so that active, on-site coaching takes place.
12) Assist the supplier in cycle time reduction by:
    - Resolving quality problems to remove the Number One rock—poor quality.
    - Improving the product yield and process up-time to assure continuous flow of product.
    - Reducing and eventually eliminating inspection and test time.
    - Reducing queue time through streamlined layout and small lots.
    - Reducing set-up time (TV tapes of current set-up sequences may help).
    - Reducing space (waste of space is as sinful as scrap).
    - Moving toward multi-skilled workers and people power.

Table 33. Traditional vs. an effective ABC analysis.

	Traditional ABC Distribution			*Effective ABC Distribution*		
	A-Items	*B-Items*	*C-Items*	*A-Items*	*B*-Items*	*C-Items*
Volume %	10%	23%	65%	10%	5%	85%
$ %	75%	20%	5%	75%	5%	20%
Receipt frequency	Weekly	Monthly	Quarterly	Daily	Daily	Quarterly
Strategy	EOQ	EOQ	EOQ	Max. inventory Turns	Min. Space	EOQ

*B Items redefined as bulky items consuming space.

WHITE-COLLAR CYCLE TIME REDUCTION

If reducing manufacturing cycle time is important to a customer or supplier company, the reduction of cycle time in white-collar, indirect labor is far, far more important. Direct labor productivity is well over 80 percent in most U.S. industries, but indirect labor productivity is estimated at less than 40 percent. Further, if productivity is measured as sales or value added per employee, the average direct labor productivity keeps rising by 2 to 3 percent per year, while indirect labor productivity has declined by 1 percent per year. With the direct labor base shrinking fast and the indirect labor payroll bloating, the U.S. faces a formidable challenge in reversing these white-collar blues. The answer lies in marshalling an assault on all indirect labor, using cycle time reduction as a battering ram.

The graphic portrayal of cycle time power. Figure 12(A) shows how cost and cycle time accumulate in a factory. The customer purchases material at some cost from his suppliers. He performs some direct labor operations on this material, which adds further cost. However, as we have seen, waiting time, set-up time, and transport time, although they add little or no cost, consume 10 to 20 times more cycle time that direct labor. Figure 12(A) portrays this quite graphically (though not to scale). Consider the area under the cost-time curve to be inventory. None of this huge inventory cost can be recovered unless the product is sold and customer payments collected through accounts receivable. Now, if cycle time is reduced by factors of 10 or more, the inventory cost will be dramatically reduced by an amount equal to the shaded area in Figure 12(A).

Manufacturing cycle time—a small fraction of indirect labor cycle time. By looking at figure 12B one can see that inventory costs in indirect labor build up in much the same way as in manufacturing. Indirect labor is expended, starting with sales, engineering, and other support services, until the new product reaches production. The only difference is that indirect labor costs are higher and start much earlier, and the cycle times are much longer than in manufacturing. Not one penny of these indirect inventory costs (the integral of the cost-time curve) is recovered until manufacturing skips the first product and receivables are collected. What an astounding cash flow problem! It has been estimated that a typical company has a negative cash flow equivalent to almost one year of sales. Again, if the indirect labor cycle time can be cut by a significant percentage (shaded area in Fig. 12(B), inventory costs will be greatly reduced and cash flow will become much less negative.

Total company cycle time—a small fraction of cycle time in the entire supply chain. Figure 12, which represents total inventory (manufacturing + indirect labor) of a company, can be equally applied to the supplier. His material price, shown as the vertical line in 12(A), is largely determined by his material cost and his total inventory (manufacturing + indirect labor), and inventory in turn is governed by his total cycle time. The same logic can be extended to the supplier's supplier and his supplier and on and on through the supply chain.

If your supplier can be encouraged to reduce his total cycle time, equal to the shaded areas of Figure 12, his inventory cost (area under the curve) will be greatly reduced and, (hopefully), he will pass on

Figure 12. The cost-cycle time curves for manufacturing and indirect labor.

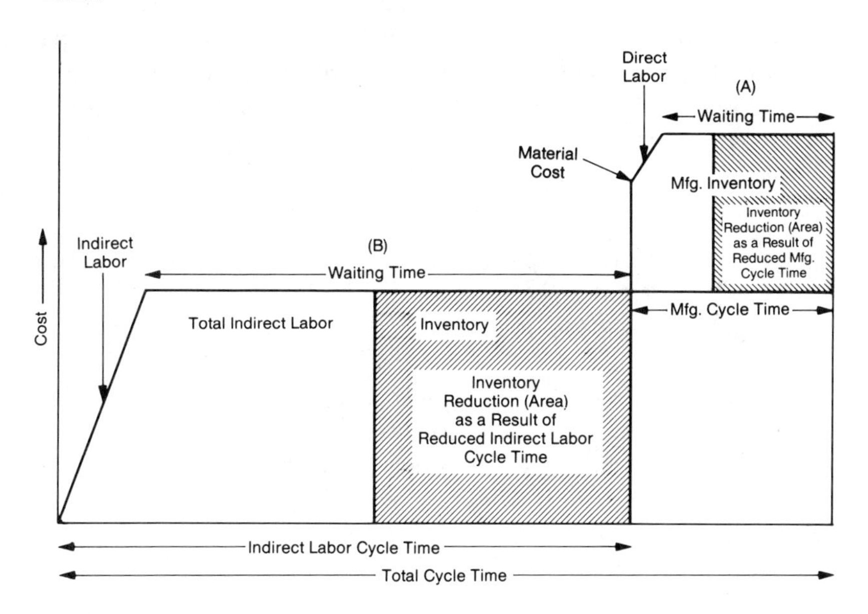

part of the savings to you. Similarly, the supplier can encourage his supplier to reduce his total cycle time, and so on, through the whole supply chain. The cumulative effects of these savings to the end customer can be dramatic. Even more important, the practice—performed as a national drive—can make the U.S. cost-competitive with any nation!

How to lasso the indirect labor cycle time bull. Indirect labor cycle time is longer and far more worthy of attention than manufacturing cycle time. But reducing indirect labor cycle time is still in its infancy.

On a long-term basis, the same systematic approach used to reduce cycle time for manufacturing can also be applied to indirect labor. The focused factory can be expanded to include all support groups, especially engineering and sales. The lay-out could facilitate a smooth flow between support departments on a line-of-sight basis. The resolution of the quality problems between these support departments could enhance continuous flows. Finally, people power is just as important, if not more important, in white collar work as it is in indirect labor operations.

Next operation as customer. There are also immediate measures that can be taken. The basic building block should be the concept of the next operation as customer. Table 34 presents a roadmap for reducing indirect labor cycle time for a single indirect labor department or for a process—especially one with major delays, costs, or quality problems—that cuts across several departments.

Reasons for variance. Problems between departments arise for one or more of the following reasons:

- poor "output" specifications from one department to its "customer" department
- poor "input" specifications from one department to its "supplier" department
- positive or negative consequences to an individual by performing or not performing a task as expected.
- positive or negative consequences to an organization by performing or not performing a task as expected.
- lack of feedback
- a poor "process" within the department
- inadequate resources

Table 34. Cycle time reduction roadmap.

A: For an indirect labor department

- Identify all functions.
- Select major functions.
- Identify "customers" of these functions.
- Prioritize eight major functions (with "customer" consent).
- Flow chart each function.
- Estimate cost and cycle time of each element in the flow chart.
- Determine importance of major elements. Assign a weight (x) by importance.
- Determine time spent by each person in the department for that element (y).
- Multiply (x) and (y) to get a profile (matrix) of importance vs. total time spent by members of the department.
- Assign a goal of 70% cycle time reduction or 30% cost reduction for each function.
- Examine the importance—time matrix.
- Challenge each element for effectiveness—for possible elimination or simplification or combining with other elements.
- Brainstorm methods to reduce cycle time.
- Evaluate those tasks that require repeating because of poor quality. Eliminate the causes for poor quality.
- Standardize, balance loads, transfer functions, improve and streamline procedures, vary skill levels.

B. For a process that cuts across several departments

The roadmap is essentially the same as for an indirect labor department (previous page), except:

> A flow chart—listing the various functions, which department performs them, who within each department performs them, and the amount of time expended—should precede the roadmap described for a department.

A cross-functional team should examine these problems to determine the best means to resolve them.

More and more pioneering U.S. companies are frontally attacking indirect labor cycle time. Their success, hopefully, can light the way for others to follow.

6

Achieving Results— A Case Study

At this stage, you may well ask whether there are any U.S.-based companies that have implemented many of the techniques presented in this briefing. The answer is "yes." Almost every U.S. company that operates on a global basis (rather than just multi-national) has launched a multi-pronged attack, using these techniques, to meet the global challenge. Space and confidentiality preclude publishing many of these efforts. However, there is one company whose achievements in the field of supply management are in the public domain.

XEROX—A BENCHMARK COMPANY IN SUPPLY MANAGEMENT

As testimony to Xerox's success in supply management, *Purchasing Magazine*, in 1985, awarded the company the prestigious Medal of Professional Excellence. In its citation, the magazine stated:

> In our view, the materials management organization at Xerox exemplifies the gutsy brand of purchasing professionalism that's a must for U.S. industry today.

Highlights of Xerox's improvement "process" include:

- Drastic pruning of the supplier base, from 5,000 in 1980 to 300 in 1985.
- Establishing a centralized commodity management with worldwide scope.
- Integrating suppliers into materials management and making them part of a synergistic team.
- Establishing closer relations with design and manufacturing engineers, with buying teams sited right in engineering to support new product development.
- Using value engineering effectively.
- Using cost targeting, with highly professional, technically oriented cost estimates.
- Involving the supplier early-on in design assistance and in the formulation of specifications.
- Setting up a supplier executive council.
- Tying purchasing goals to corporate objectives, and defining plans and tactics to achieve these goals.
- Enthusiastically adopting and improving the latest purchasing and materials tactics, techniques, and technology.
- Hiring, training, motivating, and developing professionals in materials management and quality assurance.
- Training suppliers intensively in SPC and cycle time management.

PROOF OF THE PUDDING AT XEROX

By using the techniques documented in this briefing, Xerox was able to:

- Reduce material costs by an average of 10 percent a year since 1980. This is quite an achievement considering that the material base for the cost reduction was an annual $4 billion in the reprographics group alone.
- Improve overall quality by almost 16:1 in three years, with reject levels, reduced from over 10,000 parts per million (1 percent) to 150 parts per million.

Figure 13. The dimensions of a world-class company.

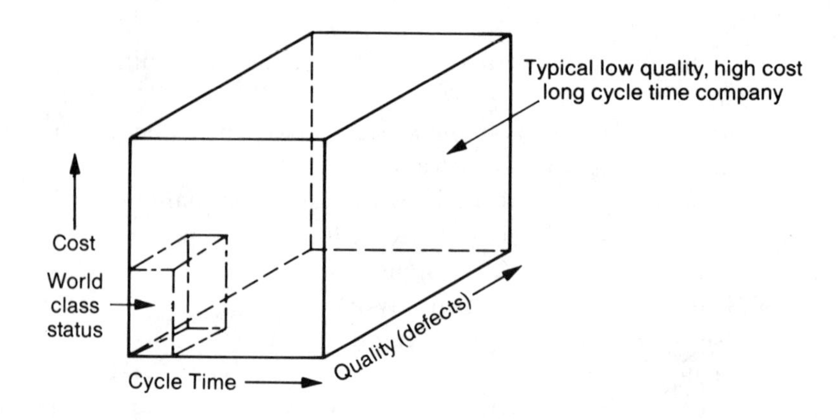

Figure 14. The large area of commonality between the quality, cost, and cycle time domains.

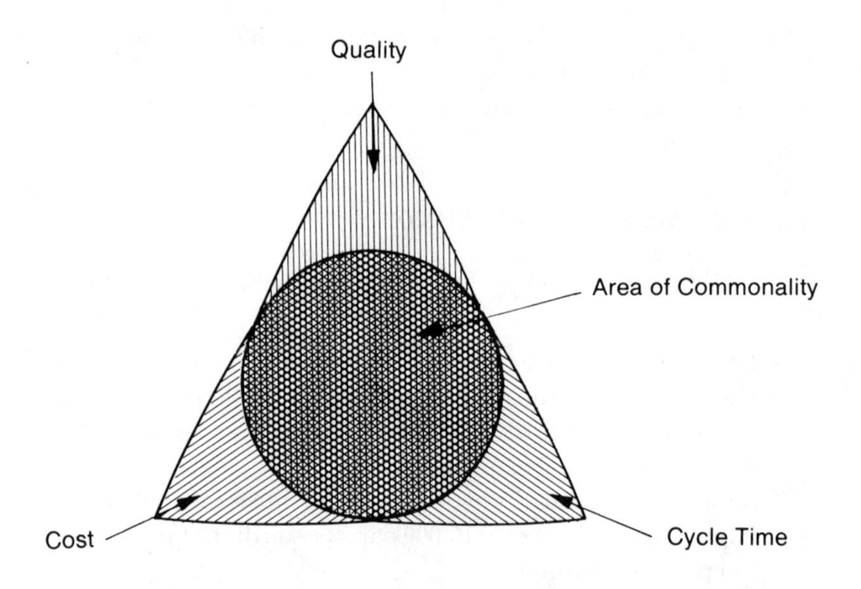

- Shrink inventory from 3.5 months in 1980 to almost 20 days in 1985.
- Reduce the cost of procurement (including materials management, supplier quality assurance, and engineering support) from 9 cents per purchased dollar to 3.5 cents in 1985.

THE MARCH TO WORLD CLASS STATUS

The quality-cost-cycle time cube for a world-class company. We have discussed three major areas for improving overall supplier performance—quality, cost, and cycle time (for direct and indirect labor). Figure 13 portrays them as three sides of a cube.

In order to achieve world-class status, you must shrink the cube toward: fewer and fewer defects, lower and lower costs, and shorter and shorter cycle times.

The conventional wisdom was that high quality, low cost, and short cycle time were incompatible, or at least mutually exclusive. Today, we know that these three parameters have a lot in common, as seen in Figure 14. Improving quality helps cost reduction; cutting cycle time helps quality, and so on in a never-ending upward spiral toward perfection—both for customer and supplier alike.

Appendix
Best-in-Class Rating (for existing and potential suppliers)

PART I

Part 1 offers a series of questionnaires to be used in evaluating and choosing your best-in-class suppliers. Before looking at the questionnaires, study the scorecard in Table A.2. Each topic in this table is covered in a separate questionnaire.

Prerequisite: The supplier's strong desire to enter into partnership.

QUESTIONNAIRE

I. Financial Strength, Experience.

1. What are the supplier's historic trends for profitability and ROI?
2. What is the supplier's market share in products supplied to the company?
3. What is/will be your company's percentage of the supplier's total sales?

Table A.1. Scorecard for evaluating suppliers.,

Evaluation Category	Weight	Rating: * (1 to 10)	Score Weight & Rating
1. Financial Strength, Strategy, and Experience	5		
2. Management Commitment to Excellence	10		
3. Design/Technology Strength	10		
4. Quality Capability—Incl. SPC	15		
5. Cost Competitiveness	10		
6. Service/Flexibility	5		
7. Manufacturing Skills	10		
8. Cycle Time Concentration	15		
9. Partnership Extension to Subsuppliers	10		
10. Employee Participative Climate.	10		
Total	100		

* Rating Scale:

1 to 3: Poor or Below Average Competitor.
4 to 6: Fair or on Par with Average Competitor.
7 to 10: Superior or Above Average Competitor.

Total Rating:

0 - 200: Poor
201 - 400: Weak
401 - 550: Marginal
551 - 700: Qualified
Over 700: Outstanding

4. Where does the supplier's product(s) to your company fall in the industry attractiveness vs. competitive position matrix?
5. What is the supplier's long-range strategic intent; what are his strategic plans?
6. Is the supplier part of a larger company? If so, what is the degree of corporate support?

7. Is the supplier likely to become a potential competitor?
8. Are the supplier's financial ratings (stock market, D & B, debt/equity ratio, etc.) strong?
9. Will the supplier be willing to enter into financial incentives and penalties with your company based upon delivery, quality, reliability, performance, and ideas?
10. What is the supplier's image in his market/industry?

QUESTIONNAIRE

II. Management Commitment to Excellence.

1. How is the supplier's management firmly committed to partnership with the company—high quality, early delivery, low cost, and low cycle time—in return for longer term contracts, larger $ volume, technical and quality help, and more stable forecasts?
2. How is the supplier's management committed to technological innovation?
3. How is the supplier's management committed to meaningful employee participation?
4. How is the supplier's management committed to extending partnerships to his suppliers?
5. Is the supplier's business/manufacturing strategy compatible with that of your company?
6. In what way does the supplier's management have a "process" to facilitate continuous improvement in all operations?
7. How is the supplier's management committed to a systematic approach to variation reduction?
8. How is the supplier's management committed to a systematic reduction in manufacturing cycle time?
9. How is the supplier's management committed to a systematic reduction in indirect labor cycle time?
10. What are the supplier's superordinate core values? How strong are its ethics?

QUESTIONNAIRE

III. Design/Technology Strength.

1. Is the supplier a world leader in the technology of current parts/products required by your company?
2. What does the supplier have in R & D capability for technological innovation for future products, processes, and materials?
3. What percentage of the sales $ of the supplier is his R & D?
4. Is there an active program for patents and other proprietary positions which can give the supplier a distinctive competence?
5. What specifically does the supplier have for its CAE/CAD/CAM/C.I.M. system that can improve his engineering and manufacturing effectiveness?
6. Can the supplier shorten his design cycle time, yet attain high production yields at reduced costs, with reduced man-hours?
7. Is the supplier willing and capable of early involvement in design with your engineering department, including specifications reviews to improve cost and quality?
8. Is the supplier's technology associated with your products in danger of being obsoleted by new and substitute technology?
9. Can the supplier link with you for electronic information and data transfer?
10. What systematic, disciplined process is in place for assuming that new products launched into production are quality effective, cost effective, and delivery effective?

QUESTIONNAIRE

IV. Quality Capability.

1. How does the supplier utilize statistical design of experiments to reduce variation in product and process design before the start of production?

2. What policy does the supplier have to measure and control variation—such as a minimum C_{PK} of 1.33 for all important product and process parameters?
3. Are key processes measured and controlled by a Positrol plan, and have key processes/workstations been certified by a process certification team, with a checklist of all peripheral quality issues that can affect the processes?
4. Are control charts—*but much preferably, precontrol*—in place to monitor key product and process parameters on an ongoing basis?
5. How are FMEAs, FTAs and Product Liability Analyses (PLA) employed on all new products to assure reliability, and are these disciplines extended beyond design to manufacturing and subsuppliers?
6. Are other reliability disciplines such as thermal scanning, derating, reliability prediction studies, or design reviews utilized on new products?
7. Is there a reliability stress discipline (preferably multiple environment overstress testing) to "smoke out" weak links in design?
8. How effective and timely is the failure analysis capability to diagnose failures down to root cause and correct them speedily and completely?
9. How effective is the teamwork between various departments—especially Engineering, Manufacturing, Quality Assurance, and Materials Management—to assure high quality, low-cost, short cycle time of new product introduction?
10. Is the concept of next operation as "customer" being utilized to improve internal supplier-customer link effectiveness in both manufacturing and all indirect labor operations?

QUESTIONNAIRE

V. Cost Competitiveness.

1. Is group technology and an associated coding system to reduce product line, models, and parts being utilized?

2. How is "reverse engineering" or competitive analysis being utilized to determine cost targets for internal and supplier use?
3. Are there professional cost estimators that can determine such cost targets with accuracy?
4. How is use made of Value Engineering as a discipline to systematically reduce costs while simultaneously improving quality?
5. Does the supplier accept an experience curve approach to multi-year pricing agreements and does he extend the same experience curve pricing approach to his suppliers?
6. Is there a systematic method of gathering, analyzing, and reducing the cost of quality, through traditional accounting practices?
7. Is there an attempt to identify and reduce the hidden costs of poor quality—which can be as high as 20 percent of sales—that are not tracked by traditional accounting systems?
8. Is there a focus on overall-or composite-yield, from one end of production to shipping, to assure a minimum of 90 percent composite yields?
9. What systematic approach is there to reducing and eventually eliminating all inspection and testing?
10. Is there an emphasis on *total cost* of procurement—including the cost of tests and failures—rather than just the purchase *price?* How is it measured.[7]

QUESTIONNAIRE

VI. Service/Flexibility.

1. Is the supplier responsive to fast-changing requirements of your company that may be necessary on occasion?
2. Does the supplier solicit constant feedback of customer satisfaction from your company?
3. Does the supplier have a short tool-making cycle time?
4. Is there early notification of quality, schedule, or cost

concerns requiring consultations with you "before the fact"?

5. Is the supplier's manufacturing capacity capable of meeting upturns in your requirements?
6. Will the supplier take on responsibility for accurate counts without the necessity of your company verifying such counts?
7. Are there likely to be possible disruptions in supplier deliveries as a result of factors such as labor unrest, non-availability of critical materials, machine breakdowns, transport problems, etc.?
8. What is the supplier's on time delivery record vs. goal?
9. Will the supplier guarantee satisfactory lead time regardless of economic conditions?
10. Does the supplier have an effective service operation in terms of diagnosis, repair, training, parts availability, etc.?

QUESTIONNAIRE

VII. Manufacturing Skills.

1. How are line operators trained in multiple and multilevel skills to achieve maximum manufacturing flexibility?
2. How are line supervisors trained in a number of disciplines, such as technical knowledge, business considerations, factory management, and people skills so that they can effectively counsel with their employees?
3. How are all levels of manufacturing trained in appropriate quality considerations—specifically systems, tools, and human factors?
4. How are all levels of manufacturing trained in short cycle time?
5. How are all levels of manufacturing trained in time studies, work flow analysis, and methods improvement?
6. Is the supplier knowledgeable about and moving toward a paperless factory in its progression toward the factory of the future?
7. Is there timely collection and analysis of data through C.I.M. or other means?

8. Is automation an end in itself or is it being used for maximum manufacturability and flexibility?
9. Is a prime consideration in automation the reduction of direct labor time or is it the removal of drudgery and worker injuries along with cost reduction?
10. What continuous program exists to reduce manufacturing overhead costs?

QUESTIONNAIRE

VIII. Cycle Time Concentration.

1. How does the supplier employ a focused factory and group technology approach to reduce cycle time?
2. Is the factory layout process-oriented or is there a straight-line product-oriented flow to minimize routing, transport, and waiting time?
3. What steps are taken in the reduction of setup time?
4. What total preventive maintenance schedule exists to prevent unscheduled, unplanned machine down-times?
5. Is there an emphasis on virtually zero defects at each workstation?
6. Is there a *pull* system of material flow rather than a *push* system?
7. Is there a linear schedule (constant production rate) to go with the pull system?
8. Is there a concentration on small lots, rather than long runs?
9. Is there a mutual agreement with your company to deliver small lots on a frequent basis?
10. Is there a similar agreement with the supplier's supplies to receive small lots just-in-time?

QUESTIONNAIRE

IX. Extension of Partnership to Subsuppliers.

1. What formal and active partnership exists between the supplier and his key suppliers?

2. How does the supplier reduce his subsupplier base?
3. How does the supplier reduce models and part numbers in his portfolio of products?
4. Is there a formal program of quality and technical assistance to the subsuppliers, especially SPC and the design of experiments?
5. Is there an extension of Just-in-Time (JIT) to the subsuppliers for both their manufacturing operations as well as indirect labor operations?
6. How does the supplier involve his subsuppliers early during the design phase of his projects?
7. How does the supplier encourage value engineering ideas from his subsuppliers?
8. Does the supplier use cost targets through reverse engineering and experience curves to establish his subsupplier pricing?
9. Does the supplier use benchmarking to select the best suppliers for each part category?
10. How does the supplier train his subsuppliers in the use of SPC, JIT, and participative management?

QUESTIONNAIRE

X. Employee Participative Climate.

1. How does the supplier use his employees' brains, rather than mostly their hands to improve the company's quality and productivity? (This is particularly applicable to the direct labor worker.)
2. How does the supplier's management encourage the active participation of all of its employees in formulating goals and strategies and in their implementation?
3. How is the supplier's management *involved* with its people, listening to them and acting on their ideas?
4. How does the supplier's management promote a climate of small, but continuous and never-ending improvement in tasks performed by its employees?

5. How is the supplier's management successful in turning its autocratic managers into participative consultants?
6. What methods are used to treat workers with respect, dignity, and trust?
7. How are the workers' achievements suitably recognized?
8. How are layoffs minimized to the greatest extent possible?
9. Is there a gain sharing (financial) plan for employees in proportion to their contribution to improvements in quality, cost, and delivery?
10. Is there a climate of "no fear" for employees to speak out and offer suggestions for improvement?

PART II

The questionnaires in Part I can be used as tools for evaluating a supplier's overall capabilities.The questionnaires in this section help to gauge a supplier's ability to manage *quality*. Again, take a look at the scorecard, Table A.2. This table serves as a guide to the questionnaires that follow and as a form for totaling scores.

Table A.2. Scorecard for evaluating supplier quality.

Organization: Date: *Subsystems*	Subsystems Ratings					SCORE
	POOR	WEAK	MARGINAL	QUALIFIED	OUTSTANDING	
	0 to 20	21 to 40	41 to 55	56 to 70	Over 75	
1. Management of the Quality System						
2. Customer Satisfaction						
3. New Product Launch						
4. Supplier Quality Assurance						
5. Process Planning and Control						
6. Production Quality Control						
7. Field Reliability						
8. Failure Analysis						
9. Quality Awareness/Training						
10. Quality Motivation						
				Total Score		

Total System Rating

0 - 200: Poor
201 - 400: Weak
401 - 550: Marginal
551 - 700: Qualified
Over 700: Outstanding

Organization:

Date:

Subsystem: Management of the Quality System

	WEIGHT (A)	RATING (R)					SCORE (A) X (R)
		POOR	WEAK	MARGINAL	QUALIFIED	OUTSTANDING	
		2	4	6	8	10	
A. Management of the Quality System							
1. Is top management *involved* (amount of time spent) in quality improvement?							
2. Does top management *actively* encourage *all* departments to shoulder their quality responsibilities, instead of just the quality departments?							
3. Is there a "quality breakthrough" management program for tackling chronic quality problems—*establishment of projects and teams for each project*, along with management guidance and progress follow-up?							
4. Are quality costs used as a primary tool for *resource allocation?* (especially prevention vs. failure costs)?							
5. Are quality costs used as a working tool (product/business managers, plant managers, etc.)?							
6. Is there a comprehensive quality system *and are its elements continually strengthened*?							
7. Are quality system audits conducted and *recommendations implemented*?							
8. Has top management instituted a *partnership program with its key suppliers*, with quality improvement as a major focus?							
9. Is the quality organization sufficiently *independent* (e.g., ability to stop shipments, shut down a line, disqualify a supplier)?							
10. Is the quality organization effective as a "coach" to all other departments?							
SUBSYSTEM RATING:	100						

Organization:

Date:

Subsystem: Customer Satisfaction

	WEIGHT (A)	RATING (R)					SCORE (A) X (R)
		POOR	WEAK	MARGINAL	QUALIFIED	OUTSTANDING	
		2	4	6	8	10	
B. Customer Satisfaction							
1. Is there a concerted attempt (market research, value research) to determine customer needs and *priorities in features (vs. cost of such features)*?							
2. Are the elements of customer *dissatisfaction* clearly identified and corrected?							
3. Is *market share* used as a measure of customer satisfaction?							
4. Are there several measures in place to measure customer satisfaction to gain an *overall customer perception* of product and service?							
5. Is quality a central marketing thrust?							
6. Is there an organization structure and focal point to *identify potential* product liability/safety hazards and prevent them?							
7. Is there sufficient contact with the customer after a sale is consummated?							
8. Is there an ombudsman or focal point to handle customer complaints?							
9. Is there an effective evaluation of competitive products, in terms of performance, cost, and reliability?							
10. Are customer/dealer/servicer councils established to obtain feedback from the field and guide policy?							
SUBSYSTEM RATING:	100						

Organization: Date: Subsystem: New Product Launch	WEIGHT (A)	RATING (R) POOR	WEAK	MARGINAL	QUALIFIED	OUTSTANDING	SCORE (A) X (R)
		2	4	6	8	10	
C. New Product Launch							
1. Are there goals, targeting (budgeting), and prediction studies for reliability, and are FMEAs prepared to probe design, manufacturing, and supplier *weaknesses*?							
2. Are *design reviews* regularly held, timely, broad-based, procedurized, and effective?							
3. Are disciplines such as value engineering, thermal analysis, derating guides, standardization, "human engineering" built-in diagnostics, ease of service, and maximum "up-time" used?							
4. Are critical components qualified, their suppliers visited, and *supplier's processes controlled*?							
5. Are there comprehensive *multiple environment overstress tests to failure*?							
6. Are *statistical engineering techniques* such as realistic tolerances, B vs. C, full factorials, component search and variables search used for design evaluation?							
7. Is there *adequate field testing* and selective market testing *ahead of full production*?							
8. Is there *early* and *meaningful involvement of production* in the design cycle?							
9. Is there a *sign-off system* on new designs by production, quality, and service organizations to assure minimum acceptable yields, reliability, and "up-time?"							
10. Is there a log of *"lessons learned,"* based on feedback from production during the pilot run and early field history?							
SUBSYSTEM RATING:	100						

Organization:

Date:

Subsystem: Supplier Quality Assurance

	WEIGHT (A)	RATING (R) POOR 2	WEAK 4	MARGINAL 6	QUALIFIED 8	OUTSTANDING 10	SCORE (A) X (R)
D. Supplier Quality Assurance							
1. Does the partnership program for key suppliers stress the supplier's responsibility to steadily improve quality, cost, delivery, and cycle time in return for the buyer's responsibility to grant long-term contracts and offer technical and quality assistance.							
2. Is there a clear policy of purchases based on *lowest life-cycle costs* rather than lowest purchase price?							
3. Are there *consultations with the supplier on design, specifications vs. cost trade-offs*, classification of parameters, and *systematic reductions in cycle time*?							
4. Is there hard evidence of the supplier's processes being in statistical control and *of reliability stress tests* being regularly conducted to verify reliability?							
5. Is there a professional, timely, and effective supplier failure analysis and corrective action capability?							
6. Are there *financial incentive/penalty programs* to encourage *supplier ideas and reliability*?							
7. Is there an effective, motivational supplier rating program?							
8. Is there a systematic policy to reduce incoming inspection from 100 percent inspection to sampling to skip lot and *eventually full certification, along with emphasis on reliability testing*?							
9. Are cost-effective sampling plans used (e.g., lot-plot plans, experience sampling, etc.)?							
10. Is there a financial recovery program from suppliers for line and field failures?							
SUBSYSTEM RATING:	100						

Organization:

Date:

Subsystem: Process Planning and Control

	WEIGHT (A)	RATING (R) POOR	WEAK	MARGINAL	QUALIFIED	OUTSTANDING	SCORE (A) X (R)
		2	4	6	8	10	
E. Process Planning and Control							
1. Are process design reviews conducted well ahead of pilot runs, especially for test equipment development and software control?							
2. Are critical process parameters identified, measured, and controlled (*Positrol program*)?							
3. Is there *certification* of the process (e.g., environment, operator instructions, work layout, equipment calibration, fast feedback of reject information, etc.)?							
4. Are operators trained and *certified* for key processes and periodically *recertified*?							
5. Are processes and inspection/tests well documented *with critical operations and checks highlighted and posted*?							
6. Are quality standards established and followed?							
7. Are statistical tools, such as *precontrol for variables*, control charts for attributes, *multi-van charts*, and *components search*, used effectively?							
8. Is there a systematic program to *reduce cycle time* by *reducing setup time, queueing time, transportation time, inspection, and test time*?							
9. Is there an accurate, timely, and disciplined test equipment calibration program?							
10. Is there sufficient research on manufacturing processes to increase productivity and quality, with a special emphasis on more effective techniques for visual inspection?							
SUBSYSTEM RATING:	100						

Organization:

Date:

Subsystem: Production Quality Control

	WEIGHT (A)	RATING (R) POOR	WEAK	MARGINAL	QUALIFIED	OUTSTANDING	SCORE (A) X (R)
		2	4	6	8	10	
F. Production Quality Control							
1. Are there quality targets at each checkpoint, and *are shut-down criteria* (when targets are not met) *enforced*?							
2. Is there a team approach of yield improvement, with measurements of *overall yield* ?							
3. Are there systematic identifications of top chronic problems, along with cost estimates, and *inter-disciplinary teams to tackle them*?							
4. Are there identifications of top, repetitive problems by product line for workers and supervision to tackle?							
5. Is there a system of parts/model traceability where needed (i.e., configuration control)?							
6. Is there an effective materials review board to identify supplier problems in production, scrap, and rework problems and move out material "holds" in incoming inspection and the line?							
7. Is significant quality data gathered, disseminated, analyzed, and acted upon in a timely, effective manner?							
8. Is effective use made of computers to rapidly gather and interpret quality data?							
9. Is 100 percent visual inspection being *changed to sample inspection, neighbor inspection, and self-inspection*?							
10. Are packing/transportation practices and operating/installation instructions reviewed to assure that product quality is not degraded?							
SUBSYSTEM RATING:	100						

Organization:

Date:

Subsystem: Field Reliability

	WEIGHT (A)	RATING (R) POOR 2	WEAK 4	MARGINAL 6	QUALIFIED 8	OUTSTANDING 10	SCORE (A) X (R)
G. Field Reliability							
1. Is there an *effective early warning system* (eg., accelerated life tests, customer plant returns, "zero time" failures, etc.) to detect, analyze, and correct failures very early in the customer's product life cycle?							
2. Are there measures to determine initial customer quality (eg., warehouse audits)?							
3. Is there a systematic gathering of field reliability data (from service stations, parts traffic, sales, service, and customer inputs) and are reviews conducted to analyze and correct field problems?							
4. Are there measurements to determine the speed and effectiveness in correcting the causes of customer dissatisfaction?							
5. Is there a *partnership program with independent dealers/servicers* to assure mutual benefit and maximum customer satisfaction?							
6. Are there special field services such as exchange programs, starter kits, newsletters with key service stations (listening posts) to improve service to the customer?							
7. Is there a company-owned network of service facilities to obtain an accurate profile of field failures and to enhance service to the customer?							
8. Are there *customer surveys* to measure the timeliness and effectiveness of company-owned and independent services?							
9. Is the parts service function meeting the needs of customers and servicers?							
10. Is there feedback to engineering *for built-in diagnostics and reducing down-time*?							
SUBSYSTEM RATING:	100						

Organization:

Date:

Subsystem: Failure Analysis

	WEIGHT (A)	RATING (R) POOR	WEAK	MARGINAL	QUALIFIED	OUTSTANDING	SCORE (A) X (R)
		2	4	6	8	10	
H. Failure Analysis							
1. Is there a systematic *reliability overstress test to failure* on each product line in production to anticipate and prevent field failures?							
2. Is there a system to return units from the field, with known time accumulations, in order to conduct overstress tests and extrapolate service life?							
3. Is there an orderly program to identify those repetitive line failures with reliability problems ("*field escape control*") to apprehend and prevent field failures?							
4. Is there a professional failure analysis capability, independent of suppliers, to pinpoint the root cause of failures in products and components?							
5. Are critical components subjected to a *destructive physical analysis (DPA)* periodically to discover construction anomalies and weaknesses?							
6. Are incoming catastrophic failures analyzed quickly and effectively to prevent line and field problems?							
7. Are there measurements to determine the *timeliness and effectiveness of line failures*?							
8. Are *tear-down audits* conducted in the plant, where inspection and test may not be able to detect potential defects?							
9. Are statistical methods such as B vs. C, accelerated tests, used to measure reliability improvements?							
10. Is there an effective feedback system of all failures to the original source of the problems?							
SUBSYSTEM RATING:	100						

Organization: Date: Subsystem: Quality Awareness/Training	WEIGHT (A)	RATING (R)					SCORE (A) X (R)
		POOR	WEAK	MARGINAL	QUALIFIED	OUTSTANDING	
		2	4	6	8	10	
I. Quality Awareness/Training							
1. Are there periodic, *longitudinal surveys* conducted among the employees to determine their perceptions of quality?							
2. Are quality system programs publicized to all personnel and are all personnel fully familiar with their quality systems roles?							
3. Is there an *error cause removal (ECR) system* in place where employees can point to sources of defects that require quick correction?							
4. Are sufficient personnel participating in professional quality society and growth programs?							
5. Are there formal quality training programs for managers, technical personnel, and line workers, *with special emphasis on statistical problem solving*?							
6. Are there formal, ongoing quality training programs for suppliers?							
7. Are there product, installation, and application training programs for services, installers, and customers?							
8. Are personnel trained in topics allied to quality, such as quality motivation, inventory control, etc.?							
9. Is statistical problem solving encouraged through *project work* and are *professional reviews of such projects* conducted?							
10. Are the results of training evaluated and quantified?							
SUBSYSTEM RATING:	100						

Organization:

Date:

Subsystem: Quality Motivation

	WEIGHT (A)	RATING (R) POOR	WEAK	MARGINAL	QUALIFIED	OUTSTANDING	SCORE (A) X (R)
		2	4	6	8	10	
J. Quality Motivation							
1. Is quality given sufficient emphasis in PMP I over and above the bonus and buy-back?							
2. *Is quality a goal within the MBOs of all departments?*							
3. Is quality given sufficient weight in the K-factor section of DMP II?							
4. Are employees rotated in their jobs to acquire broader skills and wider perspectives?							
5. Is there sufficient recognition for those who have contributed to outstanding quality work?							
6. Is there a supplier quality award program?							
7. Is there a concerted effort to win quality awards from customers and to win contracts away from competition on the basis of quality?							
8. Is there sufficient attention given to motivation factors, such as achievement, responsibility, and growth?							
9. Is there an active program of *job redesign* to convert dull and boring jobs to greater job meaningfulness and excitement?							
10. Is there a wholistic concern for the employees' personal welfare?							
SUBSYSTEM RATING:	100						

About the Author

Keki R. Bhote is senior corporate consultant for quality and productivity improvement at Motorola, Inc.

Mr. Bhote is coauthor of the textbook, *Value Analysis Methods,* published by the Hayden Publishing Company, and is authoring two additional publications in the areas of vendor quality assurance and statistical process control. In addition to serving as a seminar leader for the American Management Association, he is an associate professor at the Illinois Institute of Technology, where he teaches courses in quality control, reliability engineering, and value engineering.

He received his B.S. in telecommunications engineering from the University of Madras and his M.S. in applied physics and engineering sciences from Harvard University.

Mr. Bhote was chosen as one of six Outstanding Naturalized Citizens of Chicago by the Immigrant Service League, In 1970, he received the Zero Defects Award from the U.S. Department of Defense. In 1975, he was recognized by the United Nations Association for distinguished services to the U.N.

Note: AMA's two-day seminar on vendor quality assurance (VQA) provides an in depth treatment of many of the concepts presented in this publication. For further information, call Robert McCarten at 212 903-8210 and ask about meeting 4215.